Thomas J. Bickerton

WHAT ARE WE FIGHTING FOR?

COMING TOGETHER AROUND WHAT MATTERS MOST

Abingdon Press / Nashville

WHAT ARE WE FIGHTING FOR?
COMING TOGETHER AROUND WHAT MATTERS MOST

This book is printed on elemental chlorine-free paper.

Library of Congress Cataloging-in-Publication Data

Names: Bickerton, Thomas J., author.
Title: What are we fighting for? : coming together around what matters most /
    Thomas J. Bickerton.
Description: Nashville, Tennessee : Abingdon Press, 2016.
Identifiers: LCCN 2016005653 | ISBN 9781501815058 (pbk.)
Subjects: LCSH: Mission of the church. | Church--Unity. | Methodist
    Church--Doctrines.
Classification: LCC BV601.8 .B534 2016 | DDC 287/.6--dc23 LC record
available at http://lccn.loc.gov/2016005653

Unless otherwise noted, Scripture quotations are from the New Revised Standard Version of the Bible, copyright 1989, Division of Christian Education of the National Council of the Churches of Christ in the United States of America. Used by permission. All rights reserved.

Scripture quotations marked KJV are from The Authorized (King James) Version. Rights in the Authorized Version in the United Kingdom are vested in the Crown. Reproduced by permission of the Crown's patentee, Cambridge University Press

Scripture quotations marked *The Message* are from *THE MESSAGE.* Copyright © by Eugene H. Peterson 1993, 1994, 1995, 1996, 2000, 2001, 2002. Used by permission of Tyndale House Publishers, Inc.

16 17 18 19 20 21 22 23 24 25—10 9 8 7 6 5 4 3 2 1
MANUFACTURED IN THE UNITED STATES OF AMERICA

To my wife, Sally

*Your support, encouragement, and love
are truly the things that matter most.*

CONTENTS

INTRODUCTION:
WHAT MATTERS MOST

Each year I lead a group on a trip to England, visiting places that were important in the life and ministry of John Wesley. It is a wonderful trip, but it involves a fairly uncomfortable plane flight and an extremely uncomfortable series of coach bus rides for my six-foot-seven-inch frame. On a recent trip, I developed a sharp pain in my lower back. The pain began to shoot down both of my legs, and before I knew it I found myself in a London hospital. The diagnosis: a pulled muscle. The prescription: three pills. Still in pain after returning home, I went to see my local doctor, who prescribed more pills and physical therapy. When that didn't work, I went for an MRI and discovered that I had a herniated disk and two bulging disks. The doctor prescribed even more pills and more physical therapy.

Many well-meaning people who had had a similar problem or thought they knew exactly what I needed to do offered numerous suggestions: chiropractic adjustments, acupuncture, meditation, or something seen on TV. By this point I was just about ready to scream. Frankly, I was diagnosed out and felt as if I had taken every conceivable pill known to modern science. I just wanted to get better! Have you ever felt that way?

As a church, we United Methodists seem to be searching for a diagnosis and prescription for what ails us. We don't have to look very far to find armchair doctors who abound with answers for fixing our problem. Some encourage compromise; others suggest drastic action. The relentless bickering associated with all the rhetoric makes me feel like I did when I was searching for an answer to my back problem: there are lots of theories, plenty of experiments, and a whole lot of different diagnoses and opinions when all that's wanted is a clear prescription for how to make it better. Frankly, sometimes we are diagnosed out and just about ready to scream. *What are we fighting for?*

On the surface, this question points to the futility of our arguments and disunity. But on a deeper level, it compels us to consider what we are fighting *for*. Perhaps this question actually points us to a better alternative, a way to move beyond the discord to a hope-filled future, a breath of fresh air to rejuvenate our churches and denomination.

We tend to fight for—or pursue with passion—what matters most to us. The converse is also true. What matters most to us is typically what we fight for—what we give our greatest effort and intensity. Because this is true, it is critical for us in the church to be intentional about identifying and coming together around what matters most so that the gospel of Jesus Christ becomes a vibrant part of our lives and witness. When we focus on what matters most, our ministries flourish and bear fruit as an outgrowth of that central purpose and the church becomes a relevant and vital presence within the community. The dilemma comes when various fights, feuds, and uncertainties distract us, leaving us ineffective and mired in mediocrity. We cannot underestimate the importance of coming together around what matters most. So, the question is, *What matters most?*

In the Gospel of Matthew, Jesus left his disciples with these words of commissioning: "Go therefore and make disciples of all nations, baptizing them in the name of the Father and of the Son and of the Holy Spirit, and teaching them to obey everything that I have commanded you. And remember, I am with you always, to the end of the age" (Matthew 28:19-20). That directive is the foundation upon which the church of Jesus Christ is built and from which we as United Methodists derive our mission: "to make disciples of Jesus Christ for the transformation of the world." It could be argued that Jesus' commission is what matters most in every church—the ultimate essential. To build our life as a church around this commission means that we take seriously these key words: *go, baptize, teach,* and *remember.* But what are the supporting essentials for carrying out this mission? Because the specific ways in which the Great Commission is lived out differ from one church to another, it is important for each congregation to discern how these essentials are expressed. In the midst of this discernment process lurks the very real and ongoing temptation to lose focus. We can become distracted so easily by any number of nonessentials that, over time, can consume our energy and lead us far off the path of fulfilling this mandate. There is a fine line between focusing on what matters most and losing our focus altogether, and sometimes the line can be finer than we realize.

When there is a clear understanding of what is essential, a congregation finds purpose, meaning, and vitality. Sadly, the reverse is also true. When a church cannot discover what it is fighting for, or even why it is fighting, those congregations find themselves in confusion, irrelevancy, and decline. This is certainly the case today in our own denomination. There are United Methodist congregations growing in unlikely settings, and there are United Methodist congregations in likely settings for growth that are not reaching beyond mediocrity. What accounts for the difference? The discovery of what matters most, the courage to keep those things at the center of their life and work, and the strength to keep fighting for those things in the midst of influences that tend to distract and confuse.

When we come together around what matters most, we cherish the opportunity to connect the message of the church with a broken and hurting world and maximize our efforts in that regard. When we do not come together around what matters most, we tend to rest on our laurels of past growth or become so consumed with our internal conflicts that we never find a way to embody the gospel mandate to make disciples, let alone share it in our communities.

Becoming a vital and relevant congregation means fighting to preserve the message of Christ—a proclamation of hope in the midst of despair, joy in the midst of sorrow, and life in the midst of death. In order to preserve that message and correctly appropriate our time and energy to the training and deploying of disciples who share that message, we must find the courage to say yes to the things that are worth fighting for and no to the fighting that so easily weighs us down and distracts us. This requires intentionality, drive, focus, and constant spiritual formation. With our hearts focused on a call to make disciples, which we share as a result of our baptism, we must seek the humility and discernment necessary in order to determine the essentials that will help us fulfill this call as well as the nonessentials that we can de-emphasize.

All of this is to say there is no quick and easy fix for the challenges facing us on all levels of our life and work, both locally and denominationally. Whatever the issues might be, all are deep, complex, and real. The debates around them are furious, animated, and hurtful. The diagnoses are plentiful, confusing, and often bordering on self-interests rather than the good of the whole. Even so, the risk of letting any of these matters cancel out the grand and glorious opportunity we have to bear witness to the amazing grace of a God whose love claims us, calls us, and never lets us go is far more serious than we may realize.

We are called and mandated by Christ to boldly claim unity in the midst of diversity, forgiveness in the midst of hurt, love in the midst of hate, and peace in the midst of chaos. But when we allow nonessentials to distract us from our central purpose and mission of making disciples of Jesus Christ for the transformation of the world, we run the risk of losing everything Christ has called us to be.

How will we find our way through these days of deep disunity and great uncertainty? Where is the hope we long for, and what is the real prescription we need? What are we fighting for? How can we come together around what matters most? These are the questions we will seek to answer together.

In the chapters that follow, we will explore what's at the heart of the issues we're facing as a church, a few reminders that are foundational to set the stage for this discernment, guidelines for how we determine what is essential, a motto for how we work together in the midst of our diverse views, and thoughts about the ultimate essential, love. Each chapter will include practical stories of real people and churches who are attempting to stay centered on what matters most as they live out the ministry of making disciples of Jesus Christ for the transformation of the world.

This is not the time for us to resign ourselves to the current state of affairs in our denomination or the church at large. It is not the time for us to be reluctant to cross the river just because there are giants in the Promised Land that make our journey more complex. This is the time to determine what is essential to enable us to reclaim the power and witness of the gospel. It is the time for us to step out in faith, wade into untested waters, and cross the river, boldly believing and trusting that these uncertain places are part of God's "Promised Land."

Are you ready? Let's embark on this journey of discernment with eagerness and anticipation. Sure, there are obstacles; yes, it is hard to determine the essentials that matter most. But as the Apostle Paul said to the church in Corinth:

> *So we're not giving up. How could we! Even though on the*
> *outside it often looks like things are falling apart on us, on*
> *the inside, where God is making new life, not a day goes*
> *by without his unfolding grace. These hard times are small*

*potatoes compared to the coming good times, the lavish
celebration prepared for us. There's far more here than meets
the eye. The things we see now are here today, gone tomorrow.
But the things we can't see now will last forever.*

(2 Corinthians 4:16-18, The Message*)*

That is what we are fighting for!

1

GETTING TO THE HEART OF THE MATTER

You don't have to be a United Methodist for very long before hearing the term annual conference, which refers to a regional body, an organizational unit, *and* a yearly meeting at which clergy and laity gather for worship, fellowship, and the business of the conference. Several years ago in a session of my home annual conference we were debating the issue of morale among our clergy and within our churches. The debate regarding the source of the problem and the potential solutions was quite animated. After listening closely to the various comments, our bishop, William Boyd Grove, made a simple statement to this effect: "Friends, what we have is not a morale problem. What we have is a spiritual problem." What happened in the hallways and at the water coolers after that session adjourned was quite amazing. One would have thought that he had suggested we start a church on Mars! He was accused of being out of touch, irrelevant, and uncaring. How dare he ignore the genuine issues raised and dismiss the prescriptions offered by simply saying that we had a "spiritual problem."

Why were the bishop's words so objectionable? Perhaps it had to do with the fact that, despite the simplicity of his statement, spiritual problems are not solved easily or quickly. Spiritual problems require intensive doses of prayer, study, reflection, and conversation in order to find the renewal that is needed and desired. Spiritual problems require confession and a willingness to be wrong. Similar to the bishop's assessment several years ago, I believe that at the heart of all of the issues we're debating as a church is a spiritual problem.

WHY DO WE HAVE A SPIRITUAL PROBLEM?

Though it is tempting to seek instant answers to complex problems, it is important for us to begin at the heart of the matter and work our way to discover carefully discerned answers to complex issues. Information in the twenty-first century may be just a Google search away, but the renewal and revival of the church will require much more intentionality if we are to determine what we are fighting for while avoiding the temptation to fight for things that are peripheral or nonessential to our core purpose or mission. I'd like to suggest five I's that can help us get to the heart of the matter and understand the causes of our spiritual problem. Some are things we need more of, while others are things we need to eliminate.

Inspiration

Today the world is right at our fingertips. With the click of a remote control, computer mouse, or smartphone we are instantly exposed to the sad and frightening realities of life in this world. Tension and anxiety can assault us, causing us to post a reactionary comment on social media that reveals our deep-seeded prejudices, biases, and fears. A downward spiral can begin and spin out of control right in front of us. One thing leads to another and, before we know it, we've created a groundswell of unwise and unwarranted tension and fear.

The same thing can happen in the church. Decisions made at a meeting are texted to others before the meeting ends, creating doubts about the focus of the church. More attention is given to a report indicating a decline in worship attendance, professions of faith, and baptisms than to what God is doing in and through faithful disciples. Meetings and other gatherings begin to look more like the local civic club than a spirit-led movement of the church. Small groups spend more time discussing politics than equipping participants to share their faith with others. Far more concerns are shared during prayer time than joys. Planning sessions focus on details surrounding the fellowship supper or church supplies rather than strategies for reaching and ministering to the community. People of all ages check their phones during the sermon rather than listening intently for a message of hope, inspiration, and instruction. Before long negativity, skepticism, apathy, and a lack of vision dominate the landscape, and we run the risk of saying and doing things that cause more harm than good. In a world where distractions and bad news are right at our fingertips, we must create and maintain a church that makes inspiration and spirituality a priority so that we may come together around what matters most.

In Walt Disney's *The Many Adventures of Winnie the Pooh*, an upbeat Pooh Bear greets his friend with a hearty, "Good morning, Christopher Robin!" An equally joyful reply is shared, "Oh, Good morning, Winnie the Pooh!" But Eeyore the pessimistic donkey quickly chimes in, "If it *is* a good morning, which I doubt."[1] Spoken with a downtrodden drawl, Eeyore's negative comments temper the innocent joy and inspiration that flows so freely from the carefree Pooh Bear. Sadly, there are a number of Eeyores in the church today. They say things such as, "Oh dear, do we have to go to church again?" "Oh dear, I don't like the pastor." "Oh dear, the church is going down the tubes." Those downtrodden voices can so easily drown out the optimism, hope, or inspiration the church so desperately needs.

Who wants to attend a church filled with grumbling people and administrative discord when what's desired is a refuge from the storm, a message of hope, and meaningful fellowship among people who love and embrace others, warts and all? Who wants to associate with a denomination whose public witness at times suggests that we are more divided around certain issues than united in a passion to "reform the nation, particularly the church, and to spread scriptural holiness over the land?"[2] Who wants to be part of a church that often seems to have little good news to share and whose internal debates can potentially do more to tear down than to build up?

Our spiritual problem has something to do with a lack of inspiration. In a world filled with stories of terrorism, disease, fear, and violence, we need a refuge from the storm, a place where there is a word of hope, a feeling of joy, and a word of encouragement. Deep within my heart I believe we're all looking for a place where someone has the bold conviction to proclaim the hope that is greater than what we hear on the nightly news, a place where our precious energy and resources can be channeled into making the world a better place than it is today. Deep within my heart I long for such a place myself. We need to be inspired!

Integration

The younger generation has more to say about the subject of integration than some of us want to hear. Their fuss with today's church is that they sense a lack of connection between what we say and do on Sunday and how we live our lives Monday through Saturday. They remind us repeatedly that they do not want to associate with us if we cannot integrate the faith we proclaim into the manner in which we live.

One morning some years ago I was on my way to a nearby medical center to visit one of my church members who was having surgery. In order to get there I had to fight the early morning rush hour traffic on the interstate. As I drove along, I employed my self-imposed limit of not driving more than five miles over the speed limit. Not far down the road I encountered a semi-truck going slower than I was. I merged into the passing lane to make my way around the truck when, all of a sudden, I noticed in my rearview mirror a man who was obviously running late for work. With flashing lights and animated motions, the man attempted to get me to speed up so that he could get to his destination. Stubbornly, I maintained my speed and slowly passed the tractor-trailer. At that point, the impatient driver sped past me, giving me "the finger" in an obvious gesture of his unhappiness with my driving. To his great surprise, he realized in that moment that he had just given the finger to his pastor! The next Sunday morning, no one knew why he came to the altar to pray at the end of the service. But I knew why. And he knew why too.

This story is not just about the inevitabilities of life in the "fast lane." It has everything to do with integration. The man at the altar asked for forgiveness that day. On the days that followed, he began talking about something that was missing in his life. What he was hearing on Sunday wasn't how he was living on Monday. His rant on the interstate was being replicated in the way he was treating his colleagues, his family, and his friends. There was a lack of integration.

He knew there needed to be a change, an integration of faith with life. He started attending Bible study classes and asking more questions about how to live a Christ-like life. He eventually became a Bible study teacher, small group leader, and little league coach. He says, "My life changed the day I gave my pastor the finger!" It changed because he discovered and addressed the spiritual problem caused by a lack of integration.

When we in the church discover that there is a lack of integration between what we say we believe and how we practice our beliefs, and when we address that void with purpose and creativity, our public witness will once again have credibility.

Isolation

Life has changed dramatically in the years since World War II. With each passing decade there have been countless discoveries and advancements. Yet in the midst of this progress, there also is a sense of loss among many—a nostalgic longing for life "the way it used to be." Much has been written about the unraveling of our public life and the fracturing of our communities since the advent of interstate highways, cable television, and the World Wide Web. Some of us recall a day when front porches were a place of social gathering and you knew your neighbor's name. We might say that progress is a two-sided coin. While we celebrate advancements, some of these same developments have introduced substantial challenges to the building of community and the fostering of meaningful relationships.

Today we are more connected than ever technologically, but we are more isolated from one another relationally. Many parents, who often are accused of being out of touch, wonder about the ill effects that smartphones and video games are having on their children's ability to build meaningful and lasting relationships. As I drive through housing developments in my town, I see beautiful houses but encounter few people. Occasionally I will see a runner or walker, but as I get closer their ear buds reveal that they are isolated in their own world.

Isolation limits the development of sustaining relationships and mentors, which is essential in the navigation of a complex world filled with diverse options and opinions. It breeds the idea that all that matters is what I believe and need. Isolation also limits compassion for the basic needs of my neighbor and the dire needs of the world. In addition to lessening appreciation for diversity, isolation is a contributing factor to many of the social ills we face today. When community is lacking, we often respond by conveniently interacting only with people who share our opinion.

The same thing is true within the church. Without the development of relationships, a presence of compassion, and a deep appreciation for one another, the church, like society, will unravel and fracture. At the heart of our spiritual problem is the issue of isolation. So, what can we do?

We overcome isolation when we create opportunities for relationship and community. We are blessed when we take the time necessary to interact with people of diverse opinions and cultures. Community is enhanced when we find ways to have civil conversation and discover the goodness within people who think and act differently than we do. When we do these things, we realize that diverse people with diverse opinions can indeed serve the same God with joy and meaning. To find spiritual wholeness, we must address the issue of isolation.

Independence

In 1986 I made my first trip to Africa, visiting Liberia, Kenya, and Zimbabwe. When I was first approached about the opportunity to evaluate the mission projects our annual conference was supporting there, I was reluctant. My children were still in diapers, my church was just beginning to grow, and my perception was that global mission was the work of certain organizations, not me. Still, the opportunity continued to present itself and the funding was secured, so I accepted the invitation. What I did not realize was that this trip would change my life forever.

Over the next month we stopped at orphanages, schools, hospitals, clinics, leper colonies, and churches. At each stop, it was easy to see the poverty, hunger, and disease that the people were experiencing. In one school, the children gave up their only meal of the day so that we could eat. In a hospital, a sick patient offered a prayer for our safety. In a church, an elderly woman would not settle for anything less than offering her seat to a stranger who had come from a faraway country to visit her.

Everywhere we went we witnessed people who were poor on the surface but rich deep within. They had joy! In the hospitals, sick patients testified that they had little hope for their physical bodies but a deep belief that their spiritual bodies would reunite with God. People walked for miles to worship for hours with laughter, dancing, and singing. They had nothing to count on in their lives except a deep-seated faith in a God who would see them through. And as a result, they had joy!

With each stop I became increasingly aware of the contrast of our two cultures. I sat in the midst of people who had nothing materially but everything spiritually. I came from a place that had everything materially but struggled spiritually. We were rich in things but poor in spirit. They were poor in body, but their souls soared with joy! That simple revelation changed my life, including my whole approach to living as a Christian. It also opened my eyes to the spiritual problem of independence.

The spiritual problem of independence might be described as our desire to be in charge of our own destiny. We have been groomed by a culture that, in effect, says, "Get all you can, can all you get, and then sit on your can." We are groomed to acquire, preserve, and protect. We are taught to be financially independent. We're told that if we don't think for ourselves about ourselves, no one else will; that our securities are in the things we acquire and our self-worth is dependent upon the magnitude of those acquisitions.

I have been a part of the church since I was three days old. It is all that I have ever known. But what I encountered in Africa was a depth of spirituality that I had never before witnessed. It helped me understand more completely that dependence trumps independence any day. We need relationships with one another. More than that, we need a relationship with God. It is the only way to make it through the morass we call life.

In his teachings in Capernaum, Jesus said that if you want to be great, you have to be small. If you want to have it all, you have to give it all away. And if you want to be the best person God made you to be, you have to be a servant of all. That sacrificial mind-set creates a dependence on God to see us through the inevitable challenges that life produces. Our drive for independence tempts us to think otherwise and must be overcome if we are to come together around what matters most.

Invitation

If we're honest, we must admit that sometimes we come to church to get our batteries charged. We can get a "charge" from all sorts of things: an inspiring sermon that helps us to think about how the Bible applies to our life; a heartfelt testimony from someone whose life was transformed by the presence of God; a friendly smile or encouraging word from someone at just the right time; the loving way that a mother or father cares for a child during worship; a children's sermon that resonates more powerfully than anything else during the service. In the moment, those inspirations calm our anxieties, energize our faith, and bless us with humbling reminders of what matters most.

But what happens next? What will we do with what we have been given? What will we do with that charged battery? The answer to that question has everything to do with invitation.

By faith we are called to dis-charge our full batteries in witness and invitation. When I was serving a church, I had no greater thrill than when parishioners would say to me, "Pastor, I'd like to introduce you to my new neighbors. They just moved in last week, and I invited them to join me today." They had dis-charged their battery by inviting others to join them on the faith journey. Our churches grow when we invite neighbors, coworkers, workout partners, and others to experience what we are experiencing in church. We make disciples when we see invitation as a necessary part of the ministry each of us is called to do.

Carla was a vital member of her church. She rarely missed worship and was a faithful participant in her women's circle. She raised meaningful questions during Bible study that helped everyone understand. Her friendly spirit and magnetic smile made everyone feel at home. But the best work she ever did for her church happened in the parking lot at the local superstore where she met Teresa.

Teresa and her family were new in the community, having just relocated due to a job change. She, her husband, and their two young children knew no one in town. While they welcomed the promotion that the job change provided, they wondered how they would meet people and find their place in their new town. Little did Teresa know that the best way for that to happen would be suggested to her in a store parking lot.

Teresa had gone to the store to stock up on supplies for their new home. She found it nearly impossible to navigate two kids and a shopping cart through the aisles, let alone the busy parking lot. Carla had bought a few things that she and her husband needed and was carrying her one bag to her car when she noticed Teresa's struggle. The sight made her think of her own children and grandchildren, who had moved away several years ago.

Carla took a bold step. She approached the young mother and asked, "May I help you get your bags and your children into the car?" Dismissing any temptation to distrust a stranger, Teresa replied, "Yes, I'd be glad for you to help."

During the next few moments, Carla discovered that Teresa was new in the community and the struggle to care for her kids in this new place extended far beyond the store parking lot. It was then that Carla took another bold step. She invited Teresa and her family to church, promising to meet them in the parking lot and introduce them to others. Teresa agreed to come.

Over the next few months, Carla and her husband became the adopted grandparents of Teresa's kids. Teresa and her family became members of the church and began to build lasting and enduring relationships. They quickly moved from being strangers to friends. It all happened because of invitation.

Invitation is critical to our life and vitality as individuals and as the church. I'm always disappointed when a worship service seems to have no desired outcome, offering no invitation to let God play a role in our lives. We need the opportunity to connect the dots between what we have experienced in worship with the experiences we will have in the world. We need to be invited to do something with what we have been given. We need to be invited to consider how our lives might be different if we had a closer walk with God, and we need to extend this invitation to others. It is an invitation to walk together and discover a better way of living. I believe that part of the answer to our spiritual problem is offering constant invitations to participate in the life-changing ways of God. An invitation extended in a worship service leads to an invitation offered in a parking lot, which leads to an invitation to a new life. An inspired disciple makes disciples.

During the season of Lent, many churches in the Pittsburgh area offer a Friday fish fry as a ministry fundraiser. My wife, Sally, and I enjoy picking out a different church each Friday night and sampling the food they have to offer. We've discovered that it's also a chance to interact with new people.

One Friday night we decided to go to the fish fry at the local Roman Catholic parish. We got our meals and strategically found our place at a round table seated across from a couple we did not know. During the meal we talked about the quality of the fish, the harshness of the winter, and the latest sports news. When I asked if they were members of that congregation, they said that they attended another church in the area. Over the next several minutes they enthusiastically shared with us about their church, describing the worship services and quality of the pastor's sermons, the ways their lives had been blessed by the small group they attended, the friendliness of the people, and the growth they were experiencing with the addition of many new members. They said that their church was the "full package."

What the couple did next was a bold move. They invited us to join them the next Sunday in worship. They knew nothing about us; all they knew was that God had blessed their lives, and they wanted to do something with what they had been given. So they made an invitation.

Many of our churches are not growing, and we wonder what we are doing wrong. Perhaps it has something to do with not thinking enough about desired outcomes. Perhaps it has something to do with the need for radical hospitality, which is making sure that everyone is welcome in our churches. Perhaps it has something to do with the ability to both receive and offer to others the chance to change direction and incorporate the life-giving word of God into our lives. Perhaps the reason we have a spiritual problem has something to do with invitation.

WHAT'S THE ANSWER TO OUR SPIRITUAL PROBLEM?

When it comes to addressing our spiritual problem, the five I's can direct our focus to some key areas. However, because our human tendency is to focus more on what we're doing wrong than on what we're doing right, I want to encourage us to shift our mind-set. Perhaps what we need to keep in mind is not that we're doing so many things wrong but that we're not doing enough things right. Maybe we need to consider how the right things can become part of the fabric of our daily lives and ministry.

Just a few days after the fish fry I described, I was asked to speak at a United Methodist church in the same community as part of their "visioning" weekend. I told those in attendance about the couple we had met at the fish fry and their bold invitation for us to be a part of their church. Near the end of my speech, I drummed up enough courage to ask how much of their long-range planning was devoted to invitation. Sadly, it wasn't a part of the conversation that weekend; instead the focus was on strategies around budgets and structures and staff.

After I finished talking, a person stood up and said, "I want that couple's story to be *our* story! I want to make sure that next year at that fish fry there will be someone excited enough to tell the story of our church and invite their tablemates to join us. We want that couple's story to be our story too!"

Do you want that couple's story to be your story as well? I do. In fact, I'm counting on it! As United Methodists, we offer an open table, welcoming everyone to Holy Communion. We baptize babies because we believe that God's mighty love is offered to us long before we can utter the words *"I love you, God"* in return. We embrace a theology of grace, hope, and love that is incredibly relevant and needed in the world today. We are armed with a historical driver, set by our founder John Wesley, to "spread scriptural holiness over the land."[3] Like the couple said at the fish fry, I believe we are the "full package"!

In the midst of all the prognosticating that is taking place in the church, I believe we are missing the one element key to the whole conversation: *the need for confession and a renewed desire to seek the heart of God.*

Some would say we are at a crossroads, but I believe we are on the verge of the Promised Land! We just need enough courage to wade into the water and cross the river in order to find a land flowing with opportunity and God's abundant grace and blessing. Some want to talk about our impending death, but with all that God has given us, I'm counting on a resurrection story of new life! Maybe it's not that we are doing so much wrong. Perhaps we've just wandered around in the wilderness for forty years or so and have lost the essence of why we are a church. Maybe it's time to drum up enough courage to restore the essentials of our faith and trust God with the specifics, which we have attempted far too long on our own.

No doubt there is a lot on the line. I have never bought into the idea that our future hinges on the style of our worship, the form of our administrative structure, or some major reform that ultimately is only a theory about how things might be different. All of those conversations and more are only secondary issues that lead us away from the critical issues that will determine whether or not we will be a vital body of faith. What I do buy into is a conversation grounded in spiritual discernment that doesn't claim any one person or group has the right answer but, instead, acknowledges a genuine need for the Spirit of God to inform, bless, and forge a collaboration that will discover the right answers together.

In the midst of all the prognosticating that is taking place in the church, I believe we are missing the one element key to the whole conversation: *the need for confession and a renewed desire to seek the heart of God.* Whether or not we will be able to focus on the mission of making and nurturing disciples so that the world is transformed is dependent not on our human diagnoses and prescriptions but on our ability to humbly offer Jesus to a world that is broken and in need of hope. It is dependent solely upon our ability to empty ourselves and acknowledge that we serve a God "who by the power at work within us is able to accomplish abundantly far more than all we can ask or imagine" (Ephesians 3:20).

The answers to the issues we're facing as a church will be found in a power higher than our own—and a greater dependence on this power than we have recently demonstrated. We must be willing to endure the criticism that will come when we choose the path of addressing our spiritual problem instead of looking for a quick fix or simple prescription. It is a path that requires deep spiritual discernment and a willingness to come together around what matters most.

Are you ready to begin the journey?

2

THREE REMINDERS FOR THE JOURNEY

When I was growing up, one of my family's most anticipated events was summer vacation. Having worked hard throughout the year, my mom and dad were always very eager to hook the camper to the car and head off on our summer respite. Often we would leave at six o'clock in the evening on their last day of work and travel all night long to our destination in order to maximize every bit of vacation time possible. We just couldn't wait to get there!

On one of those all-night treks, my dad neglected to look at the gas gauge, and we wound up stranded for hours on the side of the road with an empty gas tank. On another trip, the tires were not checked before we left home, and we were sidelined with a flat tire. On another, the engine was not prepared for the journey, and we broke down when a belt snapped. In each case, the lack of advance preparation delayed our ability to reach the intended destination. In our eagerness to get there, we neglected to remind ourselves of all that we needed to do to get ready for the journey.

In our journey to discover what matters most, oftentimes we find ourselves facing a similar dilemma. We are so eager to arrive at the answers that we often fail to remind ourselves of the simple yet significant principles that are required to create an atmosphere of genuine spiritual discernment. It is important to remember that the end result or destination is attainable only if we have prepared for the journey that will get us there.

We long for the renewal and revival of the church. As we prepare to embark on a discovery of what matters most, how can we set the stage for civil dialogue and creative discernment? Let me suggest three simple yet significant reminders for the journey.

1. LIGHTEN UP, LOOSEN UP, AND HAVE A LITTLE FUN

When I became a bishop, I was frequently asked one simple question: "What is your theme?" It seemed that everywhere I turned, someone was asking that question in one way or another. The people were eager to know what my direction, emphasis, and approach would be.

Inevitably, I grew somewhat weary of the question. I still feel sorry for the poor soul who happened to catch me on the wrong day. When he asked me what my theme was, I quickly and sharply responded, "I'll tell you what my theme is: Lighten up, loosen up, and have a little fun!" Though my spontaneous remark was meant to be lighthearted and perhaps a bit facetious, I came to recognize the Holy Spirit–inspired wisdom it contains. And interestingly enough, this theme has guided and informed our work in the annual conference I serve ever since. It has been a frequent reminder of how easy it can be to take ourselves and our agendas far too seriously.

Lighten up, loosen up, and have a little fun should be a guiding principle or discipline in our quest to discern what matters most. It is a simple yet significant reminder that in order to receive the inspiration and guidance of the Holy Spirit we must be in the right frame of mind. If we have a preconceived idea or if we are unable to be flexible in the discernment of the right answer, we might just miss the surprising and enlivening inspiration of our God. Both individually and corporately, we can become so stiff, serious, and focused on finding the answers *we* desire that we miss the true answers right in front of us.

In our theology we are quick to point out that our God is a creating God who is everywhere, but in our practice we ignore this reality when we are consumed with our own passions, pursuits, and ideas. If you wonder if that applies to you, let me ask you a few questions. How open are you to course-altering inspiration from God? How inclined are you to admit that you may be wrong? How willing are you to lighten up your preoccupations, loosen up your self-generated prescriptions, and once again discover the innocent joy of your relationship with God? When we wonder where God is in the midst of the struggle we face as individuals and as the church, the simple answer is *God is everywhere.* But perhaps the more appropriate question is, *where are we?* Having minds and hearts that are open to receiving the unexpected helps us experience the amazing presence of God in our midst.

No doubt this a serious time for the church. Serious times demand serious leaders who take a serious approach to answering the questions before us. Yet one of the most important ways to discover those answers is to lighten up and allow the Spirit of the living God to touch the depths of our hearts and souls. We cannot determine what matters most unless we open ourselves completely to the one relationship that matters most.

One of the spiritual disciplines I have struggled with over the years is the art of meditation. I am a type A personality. I love to go and do. I thrive on contact with people. Yet over the years I have found that meditation is an invaluable asset in my spiritual backpack. It is a spiritual discipline that allows me to calm my soul and connect with God so that I may receive inspiration, guidance, and even rest. In the midst of all my *doing*, I have discovered how important it is just to *be*—to breathe, relax, and realize that God is greater than any problem I might face. Learning how to simply *be* is a form of lightening up, loosening up, and having a little fun. It is a way of nurturing the relationship that matters most and opening myself to God's presence.

The importance of opening ourselves to God's presence reminds me of a pastor who was fond of sharing this simple line with his colleagues in ministry: "There are no emergencies." He did not mean that there are not times of crisis or controversy. Rather, his point was that when someone believes that a crisis or controversy is catastrophic, it is important for someone else to remind him or her that there *is* a way through it. If *everything* is an emergency, then life becomes a series of tragedies—and nothing may be survivable. But if we have the mind-set that with God there essentially are no emergencies—no hopeless or insurmountable circumstances or dilemmas—then we can begin to put things into proper perspective and commit ourselves to the journey of discovering what matters most, confident that God is a constant presence within and among us, that God is not through with us yet, and that God will see us through any crisis or controversy we may face.

This does not mean that there isn't a sense of urgency to the challenges we face in the church. There is. But the urgency must not be about trying so hard to discover for ourselves what matters most that we miss the very answers God wants to help us discern. So, what are we to do?

- Lighten up and remind ourselves of the reality that God has claimed us, called us, and will not let us go.

- Loosen up and receive the encouragement of the Holy Spirit in our midst.
- Have a little fun as we discover the simple joy of being disciples of Jesus Christ.

To lighten up is to find endurance for the journey. To loosen up gives us the opportunity to breathe in the breath of God rather than dwell on the stress that grips and consumes us. To have a little fun is to realize that there is so much to celebrate in this church that we have been given to care for and serve in until Jesus comes in final victory and we feast at his heavenly banquet. These practices can become habits that prevent us from having a breakdown on the side of the road as we journey to discover what matters most. They can infuse our lives and our churches with joy, hope, and vision—drawing others to join us on the journey.

Where do we start? I think it's as simple as *lighten up, loosen up, and have a little fun.*

2. COLLABORATE, AND WHEN ALL ELSE FAILS, COLLABORATE AGAIN!

Webster's Dictionary defines the word *collaborate* this way: "to work with another person or group in order to achieve or do something."[1] While that is a clear definition, I am intrigued by what it does *not* say. Nowhere does it say that collaboration requires working with another person or group who agree with your position. In fact, the secondary definition of the word *collaborate* is "to give help to an enemy who has invaded your country during a war."[2] This is a paradigm shift for many of us: collaboration is possible when we are at odds with others—even at war.

The church is embroiled in a variety of wars these days. There is a war between the older, established members of our churches and the younger generation of Christians who are looking for meaning and purpose. While many older members cry out, "We've never done it that way before," the emerging generation counters with, "We want the church to be relevant to our needs."

Similarly, there is a war between those who adhere to religious tradition and those who advocate cultural adaptation. The traditionalists fear that everything they believe in and practice will fade away. Their battle cry is, "If you don't stand for something, you'll fall for anything!" Those wanting to see the church more intimately integrated into the needs of the community and the cultural context of the day fear that the church will fade away into a meaningless institution representing a meaningless ritual that meets the desires of some but ignores the needs of many. They say, "We have to take the church to where the people are rather than expecting them to come to us."

There also is a war in the church over our understanding of theology and how it applies in this ever-changing world. Extremists on both sides have drawn their own line in the sand and will not compromise. To the right are conservatives who believe that our doctrine is being adversely affected by cultural challenges and adaptations. They say, "Compromising our position waters down our biblical and historical understanding of the church." To the left are liberals who believe that our witness is completely dependent upon the integration of our faith with a changing world. They say, "How can we embrace our understanding of grace if our theological positions do not fully include everyone in our fellowship?" In the middle are moderates who understand both sides and are pulled and tugged, all the while hoping for a way to keep the church intact. They cry, "Why can't we all get along?"

In these days of great fear and uncertainty, it is time for us to find a way to give the secondary definition of the word *collaboration* a primary place: "to give help to an enemy who has invaded your country during a war." Though we are not enemies within the church, this is the time to adapt those words to our context and begin to cooperate with those with whom we disagree. What would it look like if we actually were to help someone who has invaded the comfort zone of our beliefs and opinions?

While it would take great courage to make ourselves vulnerable to someone who has a contrary set of beliefs and a different opinion than we do, what would an intentional act of collaboration communicate to the ones who are looking our way for leadership and hope in times of confusion and anxiety?

A key component of collaboration is deciding what matters most in framing our conversations and our disagreements. Perhaps an even more basic understanding is coming to the realization that people who think differently than we do are not wrong, only different. This is not an easy posture to take. To go to a "neutral corner" where you are required to be as open to the thoughts of others as you are to your own thoughts requires great stamina and discipline. It is a posture that must be willingly assumed rather than forced. In no way does that action water down your own beliefs or lessen the conviction with which you hold on to those beliefs. Rather, it opens the door so that you can willingly listen to others and honor those persons as gifted children of God just as you are. It is a great mark of spiritual maturity to acknowledge and believe that God has given each of us a variety of gifts and opinions. Think of the difference we can make when we find a way to collaborate and then demonstrate that collaboration with acts of grace and love toward one another!

People who think differently than we do are not wrong, only different.

Now more than ever it is important for us as people of faith to find a way to make the definition of collaboration come alive. In fact, our public witness depends on it. In our context within The United Methodist Church, collaboration is finding a way to work with persons and groups within the church to achieve and fulfill the mission of making disciples of Jesus Christ for the transformation of the world.

One of the great benefits of collaboration is creativity. Joshua Wolf Shenk wrote a fascinating article, "The Power of Two," that explains in great detail the complex work of collaboration between two of the giants in the music industry, Paul McCartney and John Lennon.[3] He says that perhaps there have never been two more opposite people to jointly create some of the most memorable music known to humanity. Geoff Emerick, who served as the principal engineer on many of The Beatles' albums, describes this unlikely pair:

> Paul was meticulous and organized: he always carried a notebook around with him, in which he methodically wrote down lyrics and chord changes in his neat handwriting. In contrast, John seemed to live in chaos: he was constantly searching for scraps of paper that he'd hurriedly scribbled ideas on. Paul was a natural communicator; John couldn't articulate his ideas well. Paul was the diplomat; John was the agitator. Paul was soft-spoken and almost unfailingly polite; John could be a right loudmouth and quite rude. Paul was willing to put in long hours to get a part right; John was impatient, always ready to move on to the next thing. Paul usually knew exactly what he wanted and would often take offense at criticism; John was much more thick-skinned and was open to hearing what others had to say. In fact, unless he felt especially strongly about something, he was usually amenable to change."[4]

John needed Paul's attention to detail and persistence. Paul needed John's chaotic, no-nonsense way of thinking. Once, in the midst of significant depression, John wrote the famous song "Help." His original result was a "slow, plain piano tune" that felt like "the moan of the blues."[5] When Paul heard it, he suggested a counter-melody, a lighthearted harmony to be sung behind the principal lyric. It fundamentally changed the song and, as a result, "Help" became a huge hit for The Beatles.

The point is this: people who think alike do not always work together to provide the best results. It may feel more comfortable to be with people who think like you do, but being lulled into sameness does not result in the kind of thinking and dreaming that breeds new ideas and possibilities. Different ideas and viewpoints create a special kind of tension that can lead to some amazing creativity. The glue that makes true creativity emerge in the midst of obvious tension is called collaboration.

In many respects, collaboration is directly tied to a word that is uniquely ours in the United Methodist family: *connectionalism*. For years now we have boasted that we are stronger together than any of us is alone. When our various gifts and talents are woven together, they form a better picture of Jesus than any one of us can create on our own. It is the combination of those gifts and talents that causes this amazing resemblance to occur. And it is collaboration that makes this likeness possible.

I know of no better example of connectionalism than our denomination's recent Imagine NO Malaria campaign to eliminate malaria-related illness and death across the globe. Some years ago our church was approached by the United Nations Foundation about the possibility of joining them in a new campaign called Nothing But Nets, which is based on the fact that the most effective means of preventing malaria is to have people sleep at night under insecticide-treated bed nets. We agreed to partner with the UN Foundation and embraced a denominational program that later became known as Imagine NO Malaria. We discovered that the slogan "Buy a Net, Save a Life" made a whole lot of sense to our people. There weren't many people who couldn't find a way to raise or contribute ten dollars to save a life. Children started selling lemonade, youth began collecting change every Sunday as an additional offering during worship, young adults began sponsoring basketball shootouts in colleges, and adults were freely giving ten-dollar bills from their wallets and purses.

Based on the enthusiastic response to this simple campaign, we knew there was more that our connectional church could do. As it grew,

Imagine NO Malaria became a much more organized effort to raise seventy-five million dollars, leaning heavily on the history of the movement and the strength of our connectionalism. Field coordinators were employed and annual conferences were approached about endorsing an intentional fund-raising campaign for the effort. But the real story of collaboration is illustrated by this amazing fact: we raised approximately seventy million dollars with an average contribution of only $87.31.[6] It takes a lot of $87.31 contributions to add up to seventy million dollars! This achievement is a shining example of the power of the connection that we United Methodists share with one another around the globe—a collaborative connection that enables us to do more together than any of us could do by ourselves.

Bishop Eben Nhiwatiwa of Zimbabwe uses a word from the Shona language to describe the true spirit of collaboration: *chabadza*. The spirit of *chabadza* works like this: If you approach a person working in a field, you do not say, "May I plow your field for you?" Instead you say, "May I help you plow your field?" *Chabadza* represents a willingness to enter into relationship with someone else on the journey. Whether "enemy" or friend, coming alongside another person to share the load of what lies ahead represents collaboration at its best.

When we have been willing to help one another in spite of our differences, our public witness as the body of Christ has effectively demonstrated that our cause— our mission—is valid and worthwhile.

Today there are voices in our denomination using the word *schism* instead of *chabadza*. They have raised the idea that perhaps it would be better if we were not together because of our differences. These thoughts about division downplay the wonderful things that unite us as a people of faith. Such conversations ignore the inspirational ways we can enter into relationship with one another in order to help plow one another's fields. With the spirit of collaboration, we United Methodists have been able to heal people around the globe both spiritually and physically in ways that would not be possible if we were not working together as a connectional body. When we have been willing to help one another in spite of our differences, our public witness as the body of Christ has effectively demonstrated that our cause—our mission—is valid and worthwhile. It is the spirit of *chabadza* at work as we partner to determine and live out what matters most.

Of course, it is hard work to find a way to collaborate. In the midst of the ongoing struggle to solve substantial issues, there will always be the temptation to seek an easier path rather than plowing the fields together. But when we take the easier path, often our lack of preparation leaves us broken down on the side of the road. And sometimes when we are stranded on the side of the road, we just want to throw our hands up and shout, "It's not worth it!" So it is important to consider what we would lose if we weren't continuing the journey together. Schism may seem to be an easy answer, but the consequences of such action would be devastating for our collaborative work of making disciples, providing spiritual and physical healing, and helping all of God's children to have the same opportunities to live long, healthy, and spiritually centered lives.

Some years ago there was a pastor who disappeared from the parish he was assigned to serve. When the district superintendent tracked him down and inquired about his absence, the pastor explained, "I went away on a spiritual retreat to discern the next direction for the church I am serving so I can announce it to my congregation." When the pastor attempted to share the results of his discernment, the immediate question he received from the members of his congregation was, "What about us? Shouldn't we be included in the discovery of what direction we follow?" You see, it is not advisable that any one person or special interest group attempts to discern the next direction for the church in isolation. We are a connected body: African, European, Philipino, and American. We are a body of conservatives, moderates, and liberals. We are a body made up of clergy and laity of all ages and stages. And that's a good thing. When we work in isolation rather than together, often the result is too many easy prescriptions and a lack of collaborative conversations centering on the real issues before us. Vision means nothing unless it is discovered in the context of community among the variety of voices that represent the presence of Christ in our midst.

What if someone does not want to collaborate? What should we do then? I believe there are four categories of people in the world, and these same categories exist in the church. First, there are those who know how to dance and dance very well. Second, there are those who know how to dance but need an Arthur Murray class to refresh their skills. Third, there are those who don't know how to dance but would like to learn. And fourth, there are those who do not know how to dance and do not wish to learn. The first three categories are fairly easy to work with, but there are those in category three, such as myself, who want to learn how to dance but will always have two left feet! The real problem, though, comes with the fourth category. What about the individuals and churches that don't know how to collaborate and have no desire to learn?

The answer is simple. You cannot force someone to dance who doesn't know how to dance and doesn't want to learn. You can pray with the hope that someone will collaborate. You can invite the individual to learn the skill of collaboration. You can even enter into exhaustive conversations about the theory, ethics, and gospel mandates for collaboration. But you can't force someone to collaborate who doesn't want to do it. A sad but appropriate illustration is the ongoing stalemate between Republicans and Democrats in Washington. The inability to cross the aisle has created an adversarial relationship that is more concerned about toeing the party line than creating a compromise that will demonstrate a deeper concern for the well-being of our country and people. The result is dysfunction in our government and a growing lack of trust in our elected leaders.

What are we to do when someone refuses to dance? It's simple: we dance with the ones who want to get out on the dance floor in order to show how we can join hands in a creative movement of unity. Our world is growing more and more desperate for illustrations of collaboration. When a conservative and a liberal kneel at an altar and pray for one another, they are dancing God's dance. When someone from the older generation sits down with someone from the emerging generation, the discovery of what they share in common creates a spirit of collaboration. When deeply spiritual people lead a Bible study during a Volunteer-in-Mission or other mission experience, those who believe that we talk more than we work see the integration of theology with practice and discover a spirit of chabadza in their midst.

In his sermon "Catholic Spirit," John Wesley spoke about the need for mutual love and collaborative work. He said,

> But although a difference in opinions or modes of worship may prevent an entire external union, yet need it prevent our union in affection? Though we cannot think alike, may we not love alike? May we not be of one heart, though we are not of one opinion? Without all doubt, we may. Herein all the children of God may unite, notwithstanding these smaller differences. These remaining as they are, they may forward one another in love and in good works.[7]

Later in the same sermon, Wesley offered this commentary on 2 Kings 10:15 (KJV):

> Is thine heart right, as my heart is with thy heart? . . . If it be, give me thine hand. I do not mean, "Be of my opinion." You need not. I do not expect nor desire it. Neither do I mean, "I will be of your opinion." I cannot. It does not depend on my choice. I can no more think than I can see or hear as I will. Keep you your opinion, I mine; and that as steadily as ever. You need not even endeavor to come over to me, or bring me over to you. I do not desire you to dispute those points, or to hear or speak one word concerning

them. Let all opinions alone on one side and the other. Only "give me thine hand."[8]

Wesley was suggesting that we find a way to collaborate together. He was asking someone to dance.

There is no doubt that the work of collaboration and connection is hard. In the midst of the hard work, some may ask, "Is this worth the effort?" I believe that preserving the mission and ministry of this vital church of ours *is* worth the effort! In fact, that's exactly what we are fighting for!

3. SEE YOURSELF AND OTHERS AS A WORK IN PROGRESS

The summer after my sophomore year in high school, I attended church camp for the first time. Having been raised in a small, blue-collar, predominantly white town in West Virginia, I was naïve about the world and its diversity. I had no idea about white privilege or racism. At camp I encountered a diverse group of youth and attended a seminar on racism. By week's end, I realized that I had much more to learn about diversity and inclusion. With new awareness of how I had benefited from the privilege of being a white male, I recognized that racism was a deep and significant problem in our world. My life was significantly shaped and formed in one short week, and I have never been the same. Attending church camp and allowing my horizons to be broadened helped me to become the person I was created to be.

I believe that no one is a self-made person. Each of us is a work in progress. If we look back on our lives, where would we be without the alterations, instructions, and revelations that others have brought to us, making us who we are today? Perhaps there was someone who just wouldn't let you go when you needed to grow in a certain way, or a mission trip that broadened your horizons in ways you never could have imagined. Regardless, someone or something shaped you, and as a result you became more of the person God made you to be. Then, just when you were tempted with the thought that you had "arrived," there was a new experience, a different learning, a fresh approach that came your way and made you a better reflection of Jesus than you were before. No one is exempt from the need to grow and change. No one.

As we embark on the journey to discover what matters most, it is important for us to prepare ourselves to be shaped by the journey in ways that we cannot anticipate. Only then are we able to receive unexpected revelations with gratitude and joy. Without this mind-set, we easily can view the journey with eyes of resentment, cynicism, and hesitancy. And if we're not careful, we can find ourselves broken down on the side of the road, once again delayed in reaching our destination.

So, what can you do to develop eager anticipation for what God has in store for you? How can you nurture the sense that you have not yet arrived at your final destination? I believe the answer is to remember that you and those around you are a work in progress.

In January of 1736, a young Anglican priest named John Wesley was on his way to America to be a missionary among the settlers and natives in Georgia. Wesley was filled with anticipation and was eager to get there. He was nurturing within himself the feeling that he was pursuing the final destination of what he was created to be—a called servant of God. What he failed to realize was that God had something more in store for him.

The journey to Georgia required a long and often challenging trip across the Atlantic from England to America. On the journey at sea, Wesley encountered a group called the Moravians, or as he often referred to them, the Germans. Wesley came to admire this devout group of Christians. Reflecting in his journal, he wrote: "They were always employed, always cheerful themselves, and in good humour with one another; they had put away all anger, and strife, and wrath, and bitterness, and clamour, and evil-speaking; they walked worthy of the vocation wherewith they were called, and adorned the Gospel of our Lord in all things."[9]

One night at sea, Wesley and this band of Moravians encountered a violent storm, throwing the ship and its passengers into an uncertain future. One can only imagine the feelings of helplessness they had felt as they embarked on a journey to a land they had never seen or experienced. The days at sea had been long and tiring. Lack of sleep had begun to affect their emotions and spirits. Now on this stormy night, their lives were hanging in the balance as the wind, rain, and sea raged.

Little did Wesley know that this disruption on the journey and these Moravians by his side would provide him with a spiritually lifesaving experience. He wrote:

> In the midst of the psalm wherewith their service began, the sea broke over, split the mainsail in pieces, covered the ship, and poured in between the decks, as if the great deep had already swallowed us up. A terrible screaming began among the English. The Germans calmly sung on. I asked one of them afterwards, "Was you not afraid?" He answered, "I thank God, no." I asked, "But were not your women and children afraid?" He replied, mildly, "No; our women and children are not afraid to die."
>
> From them I went to their crying, trembling neighbours, and pointed out to them the difference in the hour of trial, between him that feareth God, and him that feareth him not. At twelve the wind fell. This was the most glorious day which I have hitherto seen.[10]

This experience with an unexpected group of devout German Moravians had a lasting impact on Wesley, contributing to the development of his theology and the conduct of his life. He eventually came to the understanding that although the church had confirmed his call to ministry as an ordained Anglican priest, he had not yet confirmed his own conversion to God by faith. In other words, he realized that he had not already arrived but was a work in progress.

Like you and me, John Wesley was not a self-made person. The influence of this simple band of Moravians on his life was significant and transformational. He did not seek them out, but as he admitted, God provided them. As a result, this devout Anglican priest discovered a deeper, more meaningful understanding of devotion that impacted not only his own faith and spirituality but also the movement called Methodism. You might say that the Moravians were an unexpected interruption in Wesley's discovery of what mattered most. While he leaned on reason and scholarship to inform his actions, the Moravians resorted to the basics of their faith. They prayed, clung to one another, and sang songs that reminded them of what they believed. Their faithfulness created a curiosity within Wesley to know what enabled them to remain calm in the midst of the storm, and his life was never the same.

Much like Wesley's journey to America, we United Methodists are on a venture into the unknown today, and at times great storms rock the boat of our foundations, break the mast of our securities, and cause panic among us. While many of us find ourselves deeply afraid of the potentially perilous consequences of the storm and ill prepared to deal with the howling winds of uncertainty swirling around us, others seem to be able to remain calm in the midst of the storm.

I can relate on a personal level, can't you? There have been storms in my life when I've discovered that I did not yet have the kind of faith that could endure the fear I was experiencing. Yet while the storm was raging, there were those nearby who had drawn on the depths of their spirituality and had found a way to sing songs of faith while the foundations were shaking and the masts were breaking. I, like young Wesley, found myself leaning on those individuals and learning how to sing the songs of grace and hopefulness even while the storm was raging. Though I thought I had adequately prepared for the journey, I discovered that I had not yet "arrived." I was still a work in progress. I still am. Aren't you?

To embrace the simple yet significant reminder that we are all a work in progress requires humility, which enables us to accept the reality that we don't have it all figured out. It takes a strong soul to be able to say, "I was wrong," "I did not realize that," or "I need some help." The realization that we are a work in progress can come with or without our consent, but it needs to come if we are to fully discover and embrace what matters most.

Because we are a work in progress, we need one another. On our summer vacations, my father had to come to the realization that he could not always fix the car when it broke down. He needed someone else to help him arrive at the final destination. A very real temptation is to think that we have it all figured out, that we have a corner on the market of discernment, and that somehow we have discovered the road map to the way or plan of God. Resisting that temptation opens us to two amazing realizations: God may have something in store for us that we have not anticipated, and God has blessed us with companions on the journey who can help us get there.

I was blessed with the opportunity to attend college and seminary and studied under some of the greatest minds imaginable. I have learned theological concepts and, if needed, can use some very flowery and impressive language to describe what I have been taught. Yet I've discovered that there is little power in the eloquent phrases that demonstrate my academic knowledge. The real strength is found whenever I use three simple words. They are words that tell others there is a way through the storm. They are words that offer the assurance that despite the unknown twists and turns on the road, together we will find a way to reach the final destination. What are the words? *You are loved.*

When humbling or tragic times come and we find ourselves alone, afraid, and uncertain, how blessed we are when someone reminds us, "You are loved." I believe these are the three most influential words in our language, and they express a basic commitment: *I will not let you go.* When stated with grace and conviction, they are an acknowledgment that nothing "will be able to separate us from the love of God in Christ Jesus our Lord" (Romans 8:39). We need the assurance found in these three simple words when we discover along the way that we are an imperfect work in progress, and we need to offer this assurance when we realize there are others around us with the same imperfections as well.

As we seek to discover what matters most, unexpected disruptions are a natural part of the journey. While those interruptions are frustrating and, at times, unnerving, it is helpful to know that we are not alone. We are at our best when there are those who will rise up and walk with us. They are the ones who fill our tanks, change our tires, and tune up our engines. They are the ones who remind us that while discovering the essentials is not without challenge and heartache, the journey to get there is worthwhile in spite of the roadblocks we encounter. They are the ones who walk with us and never let us go.

When I was a boy, my parents took me to the local YMCA for swimming lessons. I was excited about this new adventure but frightened by the unknown of what it would take to become a swimmer. The teacher was a well-built, intimidating man who had a booming voice. He instructed us to get into the pool and line up with our faces against the edge of the pool. Our first lesson was to put our heads underneath the water and stay there until he blew his whistle. At his command, we lowered our heads under the water. It felt like minutes dragged on as I waited for the sound of the whistle. With a rush of anxiety, I raised my head above the water line prematurely. Seeing my head pop up, the teacher instructed me to go back down. I did, but as the panic inside me grew, I quickly came back up again. The teacher approached and instructed me to lower my head, and as I did, I felt the weight of his hand on top of my head. He held my head under the water for what seemed like an eternity. When he removed his hand I emerged terrified and gasping for breath. Needless to say, I never returned for another lesson.

Several years later during a family vacation, I was in a pool when a teen from one of the families traveling with us came up to me and asked if I would like to go off the diving board. When I informed him that I did not know how to swim, he took it upon himself to show me what he had learned. He paddled beside me and assured me that I could let go of my nose when my head went under water. With each passing day I could not wait to get in the water and learn the next step in the process.

On the last day of vacation, I stood on a diving board, dove proudly into the water, and swam to the other end of the pool.

What was the difference? In one instance, an instructor attempted to force me to follow his well-established rules. In the other, a friend walked beside me each step of the way, never letting me go. He knew that I was a work in progress, but he could see how much I would benefit if he befriended me on the journey.

Whether it was learning how to swim or some other experience, there were many times as a boy when I had no idea what the world was like beyond my sheltered and secluded small-town environment. I had every reason to believe that life as I knew it was representative of the world. I had every reason to think that my way was the right way. But like Wesley, God prepared for me a series of my own "Moravians" who exposed me to a broader horizon—a more complete picture—and offered me some essential pieces of the puzzle that enabled me to see the face of God more clearly.

Experiences and people are waiting for you, too, as you join others in the serious work of discovering what matters most. As I have heard many people say, "God does not call you to something that God will not provide you with the equipment to accomplish."

In the midst of these uneasy and uncertain times of discernment, it is important to remember that we have not yet arrived and that there are many more discoveries to be made along the way. You and I are a work in progress, created by God and shaped by others whom God prepares, equips, and sends to bless us each step of the way. They are the ones who remind us that God is not through with us yet. They are the ones calling us to commit ourselves to this critical part of the journey. They are the ones who reassure us that we are loved and that they will never let us go. In the great annals of time, there are a long line of them. They stretch all the way back to the one who said, "I will never leave you or forsake you" (Hebrews 13:5).

And, perhaps, they are the ones we are fighting for.

3

DISCERNING WHAT
MATTERS MOST

When it comes to determining what matters most for us as the church in this generation, the great temptation we face is wanting to get to the end result without properly and carefully laying the foundation, paving the road, and navigating the terrain. It is easy to say, "I feel this is what matters most. This is what I'm going to fight for!" It is far more difficult to earnestly search in community for what matters most and determine together how we are going to fight to maintain those principles. This search is called discernment.

Discernment is the ability to recognize or determine something that is unique or distinct. We begin teaching our children discernment from a young age, helping them recognize the difference between right and wrong. As they grow, our trust in them increases when we see them demonstrating the ability to distinguish between the two. That trust enables us to let them stay over at a friend's house, give them the keys to the car, or be lenient with a curfew. Our hope is that they will have the courage to practice discernment and do the right thing even in the midst of great temptation to do otherwise. When they do not, trust diminishes and rules increase. We long for our children to have the discipline of discernment.

I believe that God, as our creator, longs for us to develop the same discerning spirit—the ability not only to distinguish between right and wrong but also to determine those things that are worth fighting for in the midst of the complexities of our world. This process of spiritual discernment is a discipline. As you prepare to practice this discipline with others in your congregation, I'd like to suggest five guidelines that will move you in the right direction.

1. DON'T WAIT

My favorite sport is baseball. Great plays in the field, strategies of the manager, and reactions of the fans to the ebb and flow of nine innings are just a few aspects of the game that make me such an avid fan. But there is nothing more fascinating to me than watching the encounter between the pitcher and the batter.

Hitting a baseball is one of the most difficult things to do in sports. It has been noted that a fastball thrown at ninety-five to one hundred miles per hour reaches home plate in about 0.4 seconds, and that it takes a human being 0.15 seconds to blink in response to visual signals. But when a fastball is headed toward home plate, you have to do more than just blink. You have to swing the bat so that it meets the ball at precisely the right time. Porter Johnson, a physics professor at Illinois Institute of Technology in Chicago, commented, "If a person from another planet was told what's involved...they would say it's impossible."[1] When pitchers throw curveballs or mix their fastest pitches with slower ones, they can easily throw off a batter's timing. Batters often are made to look foolish when this happens and they fail to properly determine the direction or angle in which the pitch is delivered.

I have been a fan of baseball far longer than I was a player. The game seemed to start moving faster and faster, and I finally reached a point when I could no longer coordinate my reactions with all of the "moving parts" involved in hitting a good fastball. I simply found myself waiting too long to swing.

The challenge facing the church today is that "the game"—doing ministry in a rapidly changing culture—is moving faster than many of us realize. There are so many moving parts that make up a vital congregation—one that is making a significant impact in the community and the world. No one person or group has all the necessary skill sets to build a vital congregation alone. Our churches need people with technical and musical expertise in order to create a relevant and meaningful worship service. We need people with an eye for business, marketing, and fund-raising to manage the costly operation of offering Christ to a community. We must become increasingly sensitive to age, gender, race, and orientation if we are to relate to the variety of needs that each group possesses. All of these things and more are essential to making the church relevant to an increasingly diverse population. You might say that "making contact" as a church today requires great hand-eye coordination. We have to be able to see what is coming at us and be quick enough to respond if we are going to connect rather than strike out. We must not wait too long to swing!

Sadly, many churches across our country are increasingly unable to hit the pitches thrown their way. Just like me trying to hit a fastball, they have waited too long to swing—and it shows. For a baseball player, success is measured by the player's batting average, runs batted in, and on-base percentage. If those statistics do not measure up, that player soon will be demoted to the minor leagues and eventually invited to consider another career. For the church, "success" is measured through metrics such as professions of faith, baptisms, and worship attendance. Though there is important ministry and transformation going on behind the numbers, the reality is that if those statistics do not measure up, a church quickly will find itself losing vitality, focus, and even joy. Before long, the church becomes a shell of what it once was. Meetings begin to reveal the downward spiral, with conversations moving away from making disciples to meeting obligations such as the pastor's salary, utility bills, and building maintenance. If nothing changes, eventually the conversations are about whether or not to close the church.

Such conversations are becoming all too common across this country, revealing that many congregations have fallen into the habit of waiting too long. They just have not reacted quickly enough to rapidly changing times. Some have rested on their laurels of past success and have not upgraded or introduced changes in their worship, programming, or outreach. Some have denied that the world is changing and have remained so convinced of their past methods of operation that they have become irrelevant to an emerging generation. Some have leaned on the security of an endowment, never dreaming that the pool of resources would eventually dry up and run out. Some have clung to the hope that eventually people will come to their church to experience the good things they have to offer, and they have failed to create a strategy for offering those good things in places where the people are actually going. Sadly, those conversations often start with the words, "If only we had . . ."

In some of these churches, there is a real sense of anger and frustration over their current state of affairs and a deep denial of the realities they will face in the future. They have been hesitant or unable to swing at the fast pitches being thrown at them. In other churches, there is the recognition that waiting too long will result in a strikeout, and they are ready to swing into action. Perhaps even more important, they know that swinging the bat of ministry the same way they always have is now resulting in foul tips, and they are ready to learn from the past in order to discern God's next right answer for their future. This brings us to a second guideline.

2. LOOK BACK TO SEE WHAT YOU CAN LEARN FROM THE PAST

While fixating on the past is never helpful, reflecting on the past in order to determine God's next right answer for the future is an important part of the discernment process.

A few years ago I was scheduled to visit a church to discuss their impending closure. When I walked into the sanctuary, I found three ladies sitting on the front pew. They were retired but not elderly; resigned but not angry. After prayer, I started the conversation by asking them what they cherished most about their church. They recalled getting to know previous pastors, raising their children in the church, seeing those children getting married at the altar, and watching their grandchildren being baptized. They remembered the significant people who had touched their souls and influenced their spiritual lives.

After listening for a while, I shifted the conversation by asking them where they found the most enjoyment in being a part of that congregation. Instantly, all three ladies lit up, looked at one another, and responded with a laugh, "That's easy. We're all three retired teachers. The best thing we ever did in our church was Vacation Bible School." Over the next few minutes they began to describe how they had worked together each summer in years past to put on a Vacation Bible School. They talked about themes, crafts, snacks, funny stories, and the positive impact they had had on many of the kids. As they talked, their posture straightened, their countenance brightened, and their joy became undeniable. Finally, I asked them, "Do any kids still live in this community?" I already knew the answer, because on the way to the church I had been stopped several times by a school bus dropping off children at their homes. When they replied yes, I made a simple suggestion: "As a way of honoring the history of this church before it closes, why don't you ladies put on one more Vacation Bible School?"

Remarkably, they did just that! They solicited volunteers from nearby churches, put up signs throughout their rural community, and earnestly recruited teachers and participants. They met regularly to organize this one last offering—something that mattered most to them—to the God who had so richly blessed them. Approximately sixty kids showed up for their final Vacation Bible School. On the last night of the week, the church was filled with parents and kids for the closing ceremonies.

Discerning what matters most is facilitated by identifying where the key components of your church's life and witness intersect with the cherished gifts and blessings God has given you.

A few weeks later, that little church was officially closed, and those three ladies moved their membership to a nearby church. But when the doors of their church closed for the final time, they left with more joy than regret. They took with them the realization of what mattered most and the experience of that coming to life again. That experience and their joyful attitude led them to develop some vital children's ministries in their new congregation. Those ladies did more than just talk about the legacy of their church. They built upon it! And in that sense, their former congregation lives on today through the legacy they are carrying forward. What mattered most to them was not regret about the past but a possibility of what they could take with them into God's future.

Discerning what matters most is facilitated by identifying where the key components of your church's life and witness intersect with the cherished gifts and blessings God has given you. This intersection is where you are likely to discover your church's legacy. When you use your gifts, adapting them to the context of your particular ministry setting, there are remarkable and unexpected results waiting to happen—legacies waiting to be invigorated.

What are the legacies of your church that you can breathe new life into and carry forward? That conversation need not wait until your congregation is ready to close its doors. Visit the significant markers in your church's life and history, and use those places as a springboard for new and relevant possibilities. Let the example of those who were pillars of your congregation in the past propel you to be a courageous difference-maker in the lives of others. You may not be able to replicate every success where your church previously found its vitality, but you *can* replicate the spirit and determination it took to carry out those ministries and create new vitality. Even the failures that your church has experienced can be used to frame a strategy for the legacy you want to embrace and be inspired by in the days ahead. If you see those failures as an end result, you can easily lose heart and determination. But if by faith you see them as stepping stones to the discovery of what matters most and what God truly desires, those failures can propel you into the future with an attitude of expectancy and surprise. And that attitude creates the framework for a potential legacy to unfold! Once you're ready to take action and you've looked back to see what you can learn from the past, it's time to seize the opportunity before you.

3. SEIZE THE OPPORTUNITY BEFORE YOU

One of my favorite sayings is "there's a reason that windshields are larger than rearview mirrors." Can you imagine what it would be like if the opposite were true? Just think how difficult it would be to drive if the rearview mirror was as large as a windshield and the windshield was as small as a rearview mirror. The results would be devastating. There would be more crashes on the highway than we could count. We would lose our peripheral vision as well as our ability to react against oncoming traffic. Picture yourself straining to look through a small rectangular window, trying to navigate what lies ahead, while being distracted by the large rearview mirror reflecting the images of what lies behind. The mental image is almost comical. I am thankful that windshields are larger than rearview mirrors!

That's not to say that rearview mirrors are meaningless. They play a key function in helping us to be safe and responsible drivers. My car not only has a rearview mirror but also is equipped with side mirrors and a signal that warns me when vehicles enter my blind spot. These features encourage me to be mindful of where I have come from, what is behind me, and what may be sneaking up on me that I need to be prepared to face.

As we've already said, looking back is an important step in discerning what matters most. While it's dangerous for the landscape to be dominated by what lies behind us, it is important to remember the way that led us to where we are now. It is important to glance in the rearview mirror so that we can better navigate the current road we are traveling.

However, the temptation to spend more time looking behind us than looking ahead is very real—especially if we believe the past was more secure and predictable than it is today. Many of us not only want to look back; we want to go back! Remembrances of full pews, full offering plates, and full parking lots create a longing for the good old days. We dream of those days and long for them to return. Yet the reality is that there are no time machines. We can't go back. And we can be sure that if we spend too much time looking in the rearview mirror, we most certainly will crash. Changing times demand that we invest the majority of our time and energy in what lies ahead. On this journey to discern what matters most, we must be sure that we have a larger windshield than rearview mirror. We must seize the opportunity before us.

What does this mean? Let me offer a few suggestions.

Remember That God Is Not Through with Us Yet

Seizing the opportunity before us means disciplining ourselves with the reminder that God is not through with us yet. This discipline must include the truth of Jesus' words in John 14:16-18, where he promises that we will not be left as orphans but will have the gift of the Holy Spirit to accompany us. It is the conviction that we are not alone in this journey. As the writer of Hebrews wrote long ago:

> *Therefore, since we are surrounded by so great a cloud of witnesses, let us also lay aside every weight and the sin that clings so closely, and let us run with perseverance the race that is set before us, looking to Jesus the pioneer and perfecter of our faith, who for the sake of the joy that was set before him endured the cross, disregarding its shame, and has taken his seat at the right hand of the throne of God. (Hebrews 12:1-2)*

These assurances enable us to resist the temptation to long for what was and instead eagerly anticipate what lies ahead.

Keep the Light of God Aflame

Seizing the opportunity before us means keeping the light of God aflame despite the challenges confronting us. The temptations we face as a church are real, and the comparisons between past metrics and current realities reveal that we are not as strong as we once were. In the midst of all the significant challenges, we must keep the light of hope burning with conviction and possibility. As the saying goes, we may not know what the future holds, but we know who holds the future.

One of the most anticipated days of my youth was when I became old enough to be an acolyte at our church. I attended the training session, was put on the schedule, and eagerly waited for my debut. On the appointed day, the head usher urged me to stand tall, hold the taper at my hip, and walk confidently down the aisle as I carried the "light of God" into the sanctuary. The center aisle never seemed so long as it did that day, but I joyfully processed down the aisle and up the stairs to the altar table where the candlesticks were. I touched the taper to the first candle, but no matter how hard I tried, I simply could not get it to light. Little did I know that a fellow acolyte and member of my Sunday school class had snuck up front before the service and pushed the wick down into the candle, making it impossible to light!

Tears began to flow as I stood in front of the congregation, failing miserably in my role as the bearer of God's light. Suddenly, I felt a hand on my shoulder. It was the hand of a gentleman who sat on the front row of our church. Mr. Miller took out a pocketknife and found the wicks of both candles. He stood with me as I lit the candles and then walked with me—his hand still around my shoulder—as I found my assigned seat.

Bearing the light of God is an awesome right and privilege not only for acolytes but also for each of us who claims the name *Christian*. We, the church, are Christ's light bearers. Whether or not we seize the opportunity before us is greatly dependent upon our ability to keep the light of God burning in our midst and in our witness. Because there are times when we have difficulty bearing and transmitting the light—times when we struggle to move forward and seize the opportunity—it is critically important for us to be there for one another, offering comfort in our hesitancy, encouragement in our lack of self-confidence, and assurance that we are not alone in the struggle.

Assume Responsibility for the Calling We've Been Given

Seizing the opportunity before us means assuming responsibility for the calling we've been given. When I was in seminary, the bishop-in-residence was W. Kenneth Goodson. In his office there hung an oxen yoke. Jesus talked about the yoke in Matthew 11: "Take my yoke upon you, and learn from me; for I am gentle and humble in heart, and you will find rest for your souls. For my yoke is easy, and my burden is light" (vv. 29-30). Bishop Goodson used that yoke as a teaching tool to talk to us about God directing our paths, as well as the need for Christian leaders to take the yoke of Christ upon themselves in service and obedience. He became one of my most cherished mentors in the journey of ministry.

Before Bishop Goodson died, I had the privilege of visiting with him one last time. It was an emotional and stirring visit. He had grown weak and frail and was very limited in his mobility. As we talked, he confessed that his greatest struggle was no longer being able to preach. My reply was simple: "Sir, today marks the first time in our relationship where I will disagree with you. Every Sunday morning when I stand behind a pulpit, you are preaching. Your influence has been that significant. And I pledge to you that as long as I preach, you will be preaching too."

On the way home from Bishop Goodson's funeral, I stopped in an antique store and found an old oxen yoke that had been painted beet red and white. In the evenings, I would sandpaper that yoke and remember the teachings and inspiration I had received from my mentor. I refinished that yoke, and today it hangs in my office to remind me of the influence he had on my life and the legacy that I pledged to continue. For me that yoke represents a passing of the mantle, so to speak. It reminds me of my commitment to pass on the faith.

Each of us has received a legacy of faith. The mantle has been passed and placed upon our shoulders, and it is a yoke of obedience—a yoke that brings responsibility. We are called not only to cherish it but also to use it as a platform for the ministry we embrace, allowing it to inform why and how we do what we do. This precious gift from God enables us to embrace a long list of saints who have gone before us and have paved the way for us to join them in this line of splendor. It's our turn. It's our time.

I often hear persons remark, "Times are much more difficult now. It was easier to be a Christian in days past." Really? I don't know that I would want to have lived in the day of the Apostle Paul when people were killed for their faith (as many are in parts of the world today) and a massive debate took place within the church about who should and should not hear the gospel message. I would not want to have lived during the Civil War or the two World Wars, when families were split apart, warring regimes were attempting to tip the balance of power, and life was held in the balance. We often glamorize previous eras but I believe you and I were created for this generation and the unique and challenging issues we face now. This is our time, and what we do with the calling placed on our lives can influence and bless the world for generations to come.

All of this is to say that we must seize the opportunity before us in order to move boldly and confidently into the future. We dare not look into the rearview mirror too long lest we lose sight of the challenges and opportunities ahead. We must not glamorize the past or idolize those who ushered us into this present age. All we can do is use those events and persons as a platform for what we are called to do and be, as modern-day bearers of God's light. Yes, there will be times when we just can't seem to light the candle. But none of us has to bear the light alone. While some carry the light, thanks be to God there are others who carry the pocket knife and can help us. As we determine what it is that we are to do and be as the people of God in this generation, we can take courage in knowing that we are never on our own.

4. CONNECT THE DOTS

When I was a young boy, I always got excited when my mom would buy me a connect-the-dots book. I would take my pencil and move the lead from dot one to dot two to dot three. Slowly I would begin to see a picture emerge on the paper. When all the dots were connected in the proper sequence, the full picture would be revealed.

Discerning what matters most is much like connecting the dots. To see the "picture" of God's plan, we must go through the process of connecting the dots. Let's consider three important connections that must be made in order to properly set the stage for clear spiritual discernment.

Linking Passion with Belief

Today there is emotion all around us. Through social media we have the ability to instantly respond to events and issues, sharing what we think with the whole world. Those who do not exercise good discretion by thinking before they act often reveal their feelings in inappropriate posts and tweets. In those moments, even if for just an instant, those individuals have let passion trump belief.

Linking passion with belief is exercising discretion by determining what matters most. It is connecting the dots between our passions and beliefs so that our principles are congruent with our words and actions. Have you ever said, "Well, that's just the way I feel"? Feelings are real and should never be denied, but just because you feel a certain way doesn't mean that it's right or representative of what you profess to believe. In a moment of rage, you might express a feeling that is completely contrary to one of your beliefs. Sometimes when we are pressed emotionally, we begin to see that perhaps we haven't connected the dots between our passions and beliefs. If, for example, we say that we believe that the Bible is a guidebook for daily living but do not employ its principles in a consistent manner, then our belief is compromised by our lack of action.

In the process of spiritual discernment, what we say we believe must be connected to the passions that demonstrate our true belief.

Linking Belief with Action

In my first appointment as a pastor, I received a phone call from one of my parishioners asking if I would come to his home for a visit. He explained to me that he was having difficulty with his son and needed me to mediate a conversation between them. I went to their home and listened to the issues they were facing. It seemed that the boy had been suspended from school for rubbing snuff during class. After repeated attempts to discipline the child, the school had chosen to suspend him for three days. The irate father said to me, "He just won't listen to me. I have told him repeatedly to stop, but he keeps on doing it." Then, looking at his son, he said, "I have asked the preacher to come here and tell you that you need to stop this behavior!" He looked at me and waited for my reply.

Have you ever been in a situation when you had a decision to make that was not particularly easy because you knew the potential consequences of your actions? This was one of those times. After thinking for a few seconds, I said to the father, "If I were to ask you to stand up, your jeans pocket would reveal a white circle from the can of snuff that you carry around. I can't tell your son to stop something that you participate in as well." He looked at me and said, "That doesn't matter! I have told him for years, 'Don't do as I do; do as I say.'"

Don't do as I do; do as I say. This statement reveals an inability to connect the dots between belief and action. The father believed that his son should not get into the habit of using tobacco products, but his actions did not support his belief. I have a good friend who frequently says, "You can't have it both ways." I believe he's right. In discerning what matters most, we must be careful to connect belief with action.

John Wesley's journal reveals that in 1738, he was having difficulty connecting the dots between his lack of belief and his call to preach. Not wanting to be exposed for his inconsistency, Wesley inquired of Moravian missionary Peter Böhler as to what his course of action should be. Wesley asked, "But what can I preach?" Böhler replied, "Preach faith *till* you have it; and then, *because* you have it, you *will* preach faith."[2]

Sometimes the process of discerning what matters most reveals that there is a gap between what we believe and what we do. Though most often we believe first and then act, sometimes it is our actions that lead us to belief. In any case, whenever there is a disconnection between our beliefs and actions, it isn't because we don't know enough; it is because we are not practicing what we do know and believe. Are you linking what you say with what you do?

Linking Action with God

The life of Jesus provides the ultimate connection between our understanding of Scripture and our ability to live out its principles. His life connects the dots not only between the Old and New Testaments but also between the Bible and us. The best way to link our actions with the will and plan of God is to look at the witness of Jesus. Though some issues and situations we face today are not addressed through the story of Jesus, his words and behaviors provide a very good road map for our own actions. Whether it is befriending someone who falls into the category of a "loner, loser, or lost one," reminding his disciples that accepting the children is a glimpse of heaven, or instructing accusers that they can cast the first stone if they are without sin, the life of Jesus consistently provides us with a necessary connection between the sacred and the secular.

Do you remember the phrase that was popular some years ago, *What Would Jesus Do?* Though it was overused, asking this question in the midst of earnest Bible study can be a helpful way to determine how the life of Christ applies to our lives and circumstances today. What are the essentials we find in the life of Jesus? What things mattered most in his teaching and example? When we connect the answers to these questions with our own real-time situations, we determine how compatible our lives are with Christian teaching and where we need to sandpaper our souls in order to become better reflections of Jesus. Sometimes the best help we can find for connecting those dots is looking to others who are looking to Jesus.

Recently I had the joy of visiting my parents in Florida. It happened to be during spring training for my favorite baseball team, the Pittsburgh Pirates. Dad and I secured our tickets for two games. I had never been to spring training before, so I was all geared up and excited.

While we were there, to my surprise I ran into a few people I knew. But it seemed that my dad knew everyone else in the stadium! He called every concessionaire by name, and he knew every usher. It was amazing. We sat in Dad's usual area where he held court with his seatmates. It was wonderful.

On the second day, at one point in the game a woman leaned over to me and said, "You do a wonderful imitation of your dad." When I

61

asked what she meant, she said, "You are like two peas in a pod. You're just like him. It's fun to watch." As I left Florida the next day and drove up the highway, I gave God thanks that I could say with joy, "I'm Jim's son." Because my dad imitates Jesus, his life is worth imitating.

Who in your life is someone worth imitating? I pray there is someone who has helped you have faith, someone who has been a Christian role model, someone who has had a spiritual connection with you through your bond in Christ. Such people are the real deal; they have found a way to link their action with their God. They imitate Christ and because they do, we can find a way to do the same.

There is no better way to become the persons God created us to be than to link our actions with our God by imitating Jesus. Jesus is our benchmark for what is good, right, pure, honest, and true. And when we fail to live up to those standards, we can seek forgiveness from the very one we have looked to for guidance. That is the best way to get back on the right path—the path that leads to what matters most.

5. SIFT OUT THE NONESSENTIALS

So far we've determined not to wait. We've looked back to see what we can learn from the past. We've prepared to seize the opportunity before us. And we've connected the dots. Now we're ready for the final part of the process: examination, or what I call sifting.

Create in your mind a visual of someone in a kitchen sifting flour to make it just right for that delicious homemade pie that you love. No one comments favorably about a home-baked pie that doesn't have a good crust! Or image a bearded prospector kneeling by a creek side, deliberately sifting the contents in his pan in an attempt to discover that precious nugget of gold. No one will keep a few well-worn pebbles when they can "strike it rich" with a prized gem!

Sifting out the nonessentials is an important part of creating a ministry that is focused and visionary. To deliberately and intentionally sift out the things that get in the way enables a church to strike gold with ministries that are appealing and valuable.

Discerning what matters most requires sifting through all of the feelings, passions, ideas, beliefs, experiences, and actions that are brought to the table. Feelings and passions may or may not be congruent with ministry priorities. Ideas and beliefs may or may not be in alignment with Christian teaching. Experience and actions may or may not reveal that we are in tune with the will of God. The idea is to put all of these things into the sifter and turn the handle so that what remains are the things that matter most for our congregation. *How* do we do this? Let me suggest a basic tool. It is a simple question:

If _____ went away, could you still have a church?

How would you fill in the blank? Without careful examination, you might name a particular passion, feeling, belief, or action that may be important but is not *essential* for the life and growth of the body of Christ. You see, the best way to discern what matters most is to sift out the things that are nonessential. How much does a lengthy debate over the color of the carpet or the texture of the padded pews really matter? Given the fact that good people will always disagree over certain issues, is complete conformity an absolute essential? Are these the things that truly matter most in the grand plan of a congregation's ministry? Yet it is very easy and quite tempting to digress into these kinds of conversations. Before we know what has happened, emotions have deepened and our focus is lost.

To create and maintain a highly vital and meaningful ministry, we must get to the very core of who we are and what we absolutely cannot lose in the expression of our church. The problem arises when we attempt to make nonessentials an essential part of the church. The nonessentials may be important, but they are not what matters most.

63

Try asking this simple question and giving it your serious consideration—individually and within your congregation—as you discern what matters most. It will help you get to the foundation of our faith and identify the core components where we can come together and find mutual agreement and resolve. In the process, you just might discover what it is we are fighting for.

4

FILLING IN THE BLANK WITH THE ESSENTIALS

We've seen that the life of Jesus is our benchmark when discerning what matters most—the standard or measure that helps us link our actions with the will and plan of God. The idea is to connect the principles that Jesus lived and taught with the practical ways we "do church." I've suggested that asking a simple question can help us identify the essentials: *If ___4 things___ went away, could you still have a church?* Let's give it a try by filling in the blank with four things that I believe are essential to every church's life and witness—four things we find in the life of Jesus as told in the Gospels. On the surface these four things may seem to be simplistic, but I suggest they are the foundational basics of the church.

1. Grace

If grace went away, could you still have a church?

One of the greatest examples of grace in the Bible is found in the eighth chapter of the Gospel of John. Jesus was teaching in the Temple when the local religious authorities brought before him a woman who had been caught in the act of adultery. They reminded Jesus that according to the Law of Moses, the punishment for such an act was stoning a person to death. The scribes and Pharisees were looking for a way to trap Jesus with his own words. Jesus knelt down and began writing in the sand. Finally he stood and spoke these words: "Let anyone among you who is without sin be the first to throw a stone at her" (John 8:7). Jesus was not opposed to the Law of Moses. Rather, this was his way of saying that if the Law of Moses was going to be enforced, then everyone present would be found guilty. Knowing the truth of his words, the religious leaders turned and walked away. When Jesus asked the woman where her condemners were, she replied that they had departed. Jesus turned to her and said, "Neither do I condemn you. Go your way, and from now on do not sin again" (John 8:11).

This beautiful story embraces the principle of grace that we see throughout the life and witness of Jesus Christ. Grace is a hallmark of Jesus' teachings. The manner in which he offers grace in the Gospels—and in our own lives—demonstrates deep sensitivity and compassion for the error-prone tendencies of humanity. Jesus' ability to level the playing field enables everyone he encounters to have the opportunity to experience a glimmer of hope in the midst of her or his human condition.

We do not know how the story of the woman caught in adultery ends. We are not given a diary of her daily activity. We do not know what decisions she made or how her life was changed after meeting Jesus. But we do know that in that momentary encounter with Jesus, her life was sustained by grace.

Grace is defined as unmerited favor.[1] It is something that we cannot earn and do not deserve, but it is something that we can freely receive.

As United Methodists, we believe that grace is offered to us even before we can acknowledge its presence. It's what we call *prevenient* grace, or the grace that comes before. Before a child can say, "I love you, God," we believe that God has already embraced and loved that child. This is why we believe in baptizing infants. Beyond infancy, before someone ever recognizes the mistake of a wrong decision, we believe that God's desire is to offer forgiveness and another chance.

In my own life, I have always felt as if the hand of God were on my shoulder. I have often wondered why God would call someone like me to do the work I do. Have you ever felt that way? The moment we think that we are capable of determining our own fate or accomplishing something with our own skills is the very moment when we fail to recognize the gift of God's prevenient grace, a free gift that claims us and calls us in advance despite our human nature and tendencies.

We also believe that grace is always present with us. This is part of the holy mystery of God's active relationship with us in the here and now. Often someone who has lost a loved one will say, "I just don't know how I'm going to make it through this." Remarkably, though, later on the same person often will say, "I made it through, but it was only by the grace of God." While those words may border on the cliché, there is a profound truth in the sentiment. If we could see the whole story of our lives from beginning to end, I believe we would discover the significant presence of God's grace that enabled us to sustain, endure, and even thrive.

Likewise, we believe that grace will see us through to the very end of life. This is the hope we have in the compassionate presence of a God who promised to never leave us or forsake us. When his disciples were wondering about the future, Jesus said to them, "The Holy Spirit, whom the Father will send in my name, will teach you everything, and remind you of all that I have said to you. Peace I leave with you; my peace I give to you. I do not give to you as the world gives. Do not let your hearts be troubled, and do not let them be afraid" (John 14:26-27).

When my dad was a young boy, his mother and father often took him to visit his grandparents who lived on a farm in rural West Virginia. My dad fondly tells stories about his visits to the farm, though at first he did not like spending the night there because there was no indoor plumbing in the house. Going to the bathroom at night meant venturing out into the pitch darkness to the outhouse, which was located down a twisty path. Dad did not want to encounter snakes or other frightening creatures that he had conjured up in his mind.

Then one night my dad's grandmother appeared at his bedside with a kerosene lantern. She said, "Jimmie, I know that you are afraid to go out into the dark when you need to go to the outhouse. I want you to go out there with this lantern. Remember, there is just enough light in this lantern to get you to the next stone in the path."

Like the lantern that got my father to the next stone in the path, the grace of God goes before us, enabling us to get to the next step in our journey. With grace, there is an assurance that we are claimed, called, and loved with a love that will not let us go—even when we wander off the path. There is even grace when we encounter those who wish to stone us for our indiscretions. This grace was present before we ever knew it existed, is present with us in our daily walk, and will see us through to the end of our journey. While we can't see the whole story that lies in front us, God always provides us with just enough light to get to the next stone on the path.

If grace went away, could you still have a church? I believe the answer is no. Grace is essential if your church is to realize its true purpose and calling. Discerning how to embody grace as a congregation enables you to determine the specific ways you can reflect the love and grace of God to the community. Unless you take grace seriously and create ministry plans that demonstrate grace, you will find yourselves struggling with judgment and condemnation. Like the religious leaders in Jesus' day, a grace-deficient congregation begins to resort to rules, regulations, and the letter of the established "law." Before long, you might find that your church is characterized by an attitude that clearly sees the speck in someone else's eye but fails to see the log in your own (see Luke 6:41).

In 1953, Richard Blanchard became the pastor of a church in Coral Gables, Florida. When a young couple asked him to perform their marriage ceremony, he arranged to conduct premarital counseling with them. On the night of their first counseling appointment, the couple did not show up at the appointed hour. Blanchard told his secretary that he was willing to wait for thirty minutes, but then he would be leaving. To pass the time, he went to a nearby Sunday school room and sat down to play the piano—a hobby he enjoyed, along with songwriting. As he waited for the young couple, in less than thirty minutes God inspired him to write the song *Fill My Cup, Lord*, which has reached countless people with the message of God's unending, satisfying, and saving grace. He later admitted that when he was not in the mood to be used of God to exhibit grace, God was in the mood to use him nonetheless.[2]

As we discern what matters most, it is of utmost importance that we fill in the blank—and fill our cups—with God's grace so that our congregations will demonstrate grace to a hurting world. May Blanchard's words be our prayer for grace:

> Fill my cup, Lord.
> I lift it up, Lord.[3]

2. RELATIONSHIPS

If relationships went away, could you still have a church?

The effectiveness of our ministry as congregations hinges on our ability to build and sustain relationships. In fact, relationships are the foundation upon which we seek to be modern-day representatives of Jesus Christ. During worship we invite people into a new or deeper relationship with

Christ; this is the desired outcome of any vital congregation that gathers to proclaim the Word of God. After worship we build relationships through small groups, Bible studies, work teams, and neighborhood groups in order to "encourage one another and build up each other" (1 Thessalonians 5:11). When we fail to invite people into a deeper walk with Christ, inevitably we struggle to see any growth in attendance and discipleship. The absence of specific ministries that sustain and nurture relationships with others is a death knoll for any congregation.

It is hard to build meaningful relationships today. In a culture that is becoming more diverse ethnically, economically, socially, and theologically, our congregations must welcome people who represent that diversity if we are to grow. The days of homogeneous church growth are long gone. But old habits are hard to erase, and new rhythms take a great deal of courage and prayer.

There is a story often told about a wealthy man who asked a wise sage to help his son give up bad habits. The sage took the boy on a walk in a garden. As they walked, he stopped abruptly, pointed to a tiny plant, and asked the youth to pull it out. The boy held the plant between his thumb and forefinger and pulled it out. Then the wise sage asked him to pull out a bigger plant, and he pulled hard until the plant came out, roots and all. Next the sage pointed to a bush, saying, "Now pull this one out." The boy tugged and tugged, using all his strength, and finally pulled it out. Finally the sage pointed to a guava tree and said, "Now this one." The boy took hold of the trunk and pulled as hard as he could, but it would not budge. "It, it, it's impossible," the boy said, panting as he spoke. The sage quietly replied, "So it is with bad habits. When they are new, it is easy to pull them out; but once they take hold, it is impossible to uproot them."

Our struggle to establish and sustain meaningful relationships often results from the comfort zones we have established. When we see the church as a refuge from the storms that are raging around us, our congregations can become places where people who look, think, and act

70

alike gather. Once those patterns have been built, they are very difficult to deconstruct.

Often the unintended chorus in a church becomes, "We've always done it that way." Influenced by our roles, traditions, and structures, we easily can become locked into the desire to surround ourselves with like-minded people. Add to this the common misperception that we, the people of God, fall more into the category of saint than the category of sinner, and we can find it difficult to welcome the sinner, the downtrodden, the loner, and the outcast. Being comfortable with the way things are can make it challenging to invite others into relationship.

One Sunday I preached a sermon on our response to the world around us, and I used my hands as the illustration. Thrusting my hands forward, I stated, "If a homeless person were to walk into our sanctuary this morning, how many of us would use our hands to welcome this person with the right hand of fellowship?" Then, cupping my hands around my mouth, I said, "And how many of us would use our hands to whisper among one another about the homeless person's smell, dress, and behaviors?"

Much to my surprise, at that moment a scraggly, bearded gentleman walked through the side door of the church and sat down on a pew directly in front of the pulpit! After the sermon, we shared joys and concerns before a time of prayer. This unexpected visitor spoke up, saying, "I am traveling from the Midwest to a city on the East Coast. I was walking by and saw the lights on in this fine church, and I thought I would come in and see what was going on. Pray for me, please."

We prayed, sang a hymn, and had a benediction. As I walked to the back of the sanctuary to greet those who were leaving, I saw that the line of people waiting to greet their pastor was not nearly as long as the line to greet the homeless man, who stood at the other exit. The five- and ten-dollar bills that were pressed into his hands led me to believe that he just might show up again next week! To my dismay, there were some who accused me of staging this event as a part of my sermon. I had not. On that day, we were visited by a living illustration of our challenge. Would we welcome the stranger in our midst? Would we extend our fellowship to make him feel a part of our lives? Would the gospel message find its way into the actions of those who heard it? Would we invite a relationship with someone who was different than us?

Extending the offer for relationship is an essential part of who we are called to be as the people of God. Once again, the prime example of this essential is found in the witness of Jesus himself.

Jesus encountered a lot of people who operated according to the "we've always done it that way" philosophy. In the fourth chapter of John's Gospel, we see that Jesus was traveling from Judea in the south to Galilee in the north by way of Samaria, which was in the middle between the two. Jesus was simply taking the quickest route. But traveling through Samaria was highly unusual for any Jew in light of the bitter spirit that existed between the Jews and the Samaritans. The Jews believed the Samaritans were unclean sinners because they had intermarried with the Assyrians—an unforgivable act in the eyes of the Jews. All Jews, and especially rabbis, were encouraged never to touch Samaritan soil; and if they had to go through Samaria, they were not to speak to the unclean people who lived there.

Jesus, a Jewish rabbi, was not only in Samaria; he was talking to a Samaritan. To make matters worse, he was talking to a Samaritan *woman*. In those days it was considered unfortunate to be born female. They only thing a woman was considered good for was reproduction. Men were not even to talk to women on the street. It just wasn't decent.

Here Jesus was talking to a Samaritan woman on unclean soil. It was highly unusual and very unacceptable for him to invite a relationship with such a person in such a place. Yet that was just like Jesus.

Not only did the Jews consider this interaction between races taboo but Samaritans themselves had come to expect the treatment they so often received. So it's understandable that when Jesus asked for a drink, the woman replied, "Hey, wait a minute. I am a Samaritan. You are a Jew. How is it that you ask a drink from me?" (John 4:9, author's paraphrase).

Jesus did not have to pass through Samaria. He did not have to take the initiative and invite the relationship. But a study of the behavioral patterns of Jesus reveals that warmth and sympathy were a part of his demeanor. He was never too proud or too good to speak and associate with those who were considered undesirable. In a day of Pharisaic laws centered on correct behavior, Jesus was a nonconformist.

This story shows the great character of Jesus, the Christ. He hung out with people who were outcast by society. Because he broke down social barriers and talked when no one else dared, he opened a door that enabled this woman to see the truth of the gospel of love. Jesus treated her not as a Samaritan but as a human being worthy of love and care. He accepted her, and through that acceptance he demonstrated that one of the things that matters most is relationships.

This story represents one of the greatest challenges on the Christian journey. Can we love people as Jesus did? Can we find the courage to step beyond our comfort zones and venture into the world to love those who are different than us? We freely use the word *Christian*, but do we really understand what it means? Webster's Dictionary defines a Christian not only as "one who professes belief in the teachings of Jesus Christ" but also as someone who is characterized by "treating other people in a kind and generous way."[4] As followers of Christ, will we choose to treat others with the kindness and generosity he demonstrated?

What helps us choose the kind and loving response is the presence of Christ within us. Looking to Jesus and his example can guide us to work out our stories with our Christian faith rather than *in spite of* our Christian faith. Our faith should be evident in every situation and with every individual we encounter. Yet that is possible only when we cultivate a deep relationship with Jesus. A meaningful relationship with Jesus gives the courage we need to build relationships with others. It's all about relationship.

Two boys left home to venture into the world. They first went to a hermit and requested philosophies for their lives. "How do you see people?" the hermit asked them. One boy said that, in his opinion, people were self-centered, greedy, and cynical. The other boy said that he felt people were good, kind, sincere, and full of love. The hermit replied, "The people out in the world will readily be the same, for each individual is the key to how he or she will find the other person."

> Our faith should be evident in every situation and with every individual we encounter. Yet that is possible only when we cultivate a deep relationship with Jesus.

Jesus found the woman at the well as a person who could love and be loved, care and be cared for, in spite of her status as defined by the world. When we cultivate a relationship with Jesus, we begin to see others as he did.

When I was a youth pastor, there was a man in the church where I served who was a whistler. He was a happy-go-lucky sort of man whose life was a real witness to his joyful whistle. He treated everyone with kindness. Every day he whistled the hymns from the previous Sunday's service. He helped me see the joy of Christ. I remember his name like it was my own.

There was another man in that church who had a business right next to that of the whistler. This man did nothing but complain, gripe, fuss, and blow hot air about anything that was done, whether it was in a church meeting or in his business. He was what my family calls a grumble-butt. It's funny, but for the life of me, I can't remember his name.

Every day we have the choice to be a whistler or a whiner. We can extend the offer for a relationship with others, or we can hide away in the established cocoons of our existence. What matters most to us will determine which choice we make.

I have chosen to be a follower of Jesus. I have been converted to this way of life because of an offer made to me years ago—an offer for a relationship with Jesus. I believe so much in this relationship that I fully embrace the Wesleyan idea of striving for perfection or sanctification, which is becoming more and more like Christ. I want to have the mind and heart of Jesus and to devote my life to attaining Christlike holiness. Don't you? If we do, then we must fill in the blank of what matters most with the word *relationship*.

One day Jesus offered the woman at the well a relationship. How might we do the same? As our relationship with Jesus unfolds, we continue to discover the courage to build relationships with the world and its people. Our ability to invite others into relationship—with Christ and with one another—will be a determining factor of the health and vitality of our congregations.

3. JOY

If joy went away, could you still have a church?

In all of my work with churches through the years, the word that seems to be the hardest for many congregations to fill in the blank is *joy*. Joy is a challenge for many of us because of the uncertainty and fear we have about the future. Fear has many ways of expressing itself in the human soul. It can be the root cause of things such as anger, stubbornness, paralysis, and apathy; and it most certainly is a contributing factor in the absence of joy.

Years ago visitors would try out a church for several weeks before determining whether or not to associate with that particular community of faith. Today we generally have one chance to make a good impression with visitors, and having a poor reputation in the community cancels out that one chance. When working with churches, I often put myself in the shoes of a potential visitor and create a mental checklist of things that would keep me from returning for another service. I might be able to overlook mediocre music or an average sermon. The length of the service might concern me a bit, as would the amount of planning that went into the service. But those would not be at the top of my list. The number one thing on my mental checklist that would prevent me from returning is the absence of joy.

In the Gospel of John, after Jesus washed the feet of his disciples and foretold his impending death, he began to instruct this motley crew of followers with some of the most cherished words ever recorded in human history. He urged them not to be troubled but to trust in God's enduring presence. He promised them that they would not be orphaned and left alone. He assured them of the gift of the Holy Spirit to guide them into the future. He reminded them to abide in his presence and follow the commandment of love. Then, in chapter 15, he spoke one beautiful line that captures the essence of who he was and what he came to proclaim: "I have said these things to you so that my joy may be in you, and that your joy may be complete" (John 15:11). Jesus' mission statement was all about joy—complete joy!

One of the staff members in the office of our annual conference has a young daughter who often joins her mom at the office. One day I was heading back to talk with this staff member when I caught a glimpse of her little girl. I noticed her, but she didn't see me. She was having the best time making silly faces, singing a song, and dancing a little dance.

Suddenly she spotted me. Immediately she stopped dead in her tracks! She giggled when our eyes met, and then quickly we both turned and went on with our activities. Later in the day I became very disappointed in myself. I should have stopped and danced with her! The invitation to dance had been right in front of me, and I had missed it.

The problem is not that we are never invited to dance. The problem is that we are so addicted to living (moving from one moment to the next, making the next appointment, striving for the next goal) and so consumed with what frightens us (what people might think, who might take advantage of us, how we might be criticized) that we miss the opportunity to dance—and even run the risk of forgetting *how* to dance. What is truly at risk is our ability to express pure, innocent, God-given joy.

There are two categories of our existence. We live, and we wait to live. If we're honest, we spend most of our lives waiting to live. We wait to live as we drive, stand in line, work on the latest task, worry about something that might happen, or process our anger or disappointment over something that has happened. But like that staff member's daughter, the little children in our lives tend to simply live. Overall they are innocent, happy, and joyful. Their lives are an invitation for us to dance in the midst of the pain and tension that so often are part of life.

Joy in the happiest child we can imagine is only a fraction of the joy that God possesses. Joy is central to the heart of God, and God's joy is as full as it can be! As Jesus said, God's desire is for our joy to be full, too—complete. What would complete joy look like in your life? What would it look like in your church?

The problem is not that we are too happy and need to be more serious. The problem is that we are too serious and will not allow ourselves to be truly happy. When my kids were small, it didn't matter whether I made a funny face or silly sound or initiated some crazy, spontaneous game. When I would finish, my children would say, "Do it again, Daddy. Do it again." And I would—over and over and over again. Why? Because of the joy that it brought to them and to me.

In his book *Orthodoxy*, G. K. Chesterton wrote:

> Grown-up people are not strong enough to exult in monotony. But perhaps God is strong enough to exult in monotony. It is possible that God says every morning, "Do it again" to the sun; and every evening, "Do it again" to the moon. It may not be automatic necessity that makes all daisies alike; it may be that God makes every daisy separately, but has never got tired of making them. It may be that He has the eternal appetite of infancy; for we have sinned and grown old, and our Father is younger than we.[5]

God's joy is on display every fall when the leaves change, every winter when the snow falls, every spring when the flowers bloom, and every summer when the plants bear fruit. The same cycles happen in nature millennium after millennium, and it appears that our God has not grown tired of any of it because God has an infinite capacity for joy.

When my wife, Sally, and I were dating, I would say good night to her at the steps leading up to her front door. Sally discovered that standing on the first step gave her the height to be able to look me in the eyes. On date nights the ritual was for her to climb the step, turn around, and kiss me good night. Since those days we have been married for many years and have found a rhythm to our life together. But to this day, whenever we are alone climbing steps somewhere, she often will get ahead of me, turn around, and give me a kiss. This action that began when we started dating has been replicated over and over but has never lost its meaning, because it is a joy-filled reminder of the love that we share.

I am convinced that many problems in our world today exist because once-meaningful acts or events have lost their joy—and hence their significance and vitality. The same could be said for many of the problems we are experiencing in our churches. Habits have grown old. Honored traditions have lost their meaning. The mechanics of worship and ministry have replaced the spontaneity that breeds a deep sense of joy and satisfaction. As Chesterton suggests, "We have sinned and grown old, and our Father is younger than we."[6]

Our source of joy and vitality is God. Have you ever thought what the first chapter of Genesis would look like if there had been no joy in the act of creation? It might look something like this:

> In the beginning it was 9:00 a.m. and God had to go to work. God filled out a work order to separate the light from the darkness. God contemplated putting stars in the heavens but considered it to be too much work. Besides, God said, "It's not my job." God decided to knock off early and call it a day. And when God looked at all that God had done, he said, "Eh, it'll have to do."
>
> The second day, God separated the water from dry land and made all dry land flat, plain, and functional. As a result, the whole earth looked like a strip mall parking lot. God thought about making mountains, valleys, glaciers, jungles, and forests but

decided that it wasn't worth the effort. And God looked at all God had done and said, "Eh, it'll have to do."

On the third day, God made a pigeon to fly, a carp to swim, and a cat to creep. God thought about making other species of animals in all sizes and shapes, but God couldn't drum up any enthusiasm. In fact, God wasn't too crazy about the cat. Besides that, it was almost time for Jimmy Fallon. And God looked at all God had done and said, "Eh, it'll have to do."

At the end of the week, God was seriously burned out. Breathing a big sigh of relief, God said, "Thank me, it's Friday." And that was the end of the story.

We all know that Genesis looks nothing like this. Genesis tells us that God spoke and it was so, and God said it was good. God took great joy in the work of God's hands. On the first day of creation, God separated the light from the darkness. It happened again on the second day. It has happened every day since then, and it appears that God has never grown tired of doing it.

"Melancholy should be an innocent interlude, a tender and fugitive frame of mind; praise should be the permanent pulsation of the soul. Pessimism is at best an emotional half-holiday; joy is the uproarious labour by which all things live....Joy, which was the small publicity of the pagan, is the gigantic secret of the Christian."[7] —G. K. Chesterton

---

We in the church are representatives of the creator or author of happiness. We are the keepers of the accounts that tell the story of God's joy. Joy is essential if we are going to replicate God's presence in the communities we serve. What radiates from the walls of our churches and the testimonies of our lives will determine how people perceive and understand God in their midst. If what they see and experience is fear, anger, apathy, and boredom, they will not want to follow the God we represent.

This does not mean that we should downplay sadness and heartache. Jesus himself was described as man of sorrow and acquainted with grief (Isaiah 53:3). But joy is God's eternal desire and basic declaration. In Luke 15, Jesus tells the story of the lost sheep, the lost coin, and the lost son. In the midst of these illustrations, Jesus declares, "Just so, I tell you, there will be more joy in heaven over one sinner who repents than over ninety-nine righteous persons who need no repentance" (Luke 15:7). Anytime that anyone lives, God is joyful! Every time somebody gets it right, God rejoices!

We were made for joy. It is why we were created. If joy is not an essential part of our life and work as the church, we have missed one of the foundational reasons for our being. Yet often we have a difficult time embracing this basic, fundamental concept. Some of us are joy challenged and have to fight against the tendency to be overly negative and highly skeptical. And because of this, some of our congregations are severely joy impaired.

In his book *Letters to Malcolm: Chiefly on Prayer*, C. S. Lewis says that while dance and games may seem frivolous and unimportant amidst the many concerns of this life, they are not frivolous at all in heaven. He writes, "Joy is the serious business of Heaven."[8] What a wonderful concept! Because joy is the serious business of heaven, it deserves to be actively pursued and practiced in our lives and our congregations. Joy is essential if we are to accurately embody God in our midst.

Though we may affirm the importance of joy, the challenges to pursuing joy are real. We tend to think we will be happy when our conditions change. It is the dilemma of the human condition.

The truth is that we do not find joy when our circumstances change; we find it in the midst of our circumstances. In fact, often it is when we are suffering that we discover an unshakable, powerful joy! One of the tests of authentic joy is that it is compatible with and present in the midst of pain. To delay joy until things improve ensures that joy will never come or will be short-lived. Joy in this life is nearly always joy in spite of something.

Life isn't perfect. Your spouse, kids, relatives, in-laws, friends, neighbors, and coworkers will never be perfect. And most assuredly there is no church anywhere in the world that is perfect. If we are going to embrace joy, now is the time.

Psalm 118:24 says, "This is the day the LORD has made; let us rejoice and be glad in it." Today is the day to rejoice! Today is the day to dance! If we are to represent God well, it is essential for us to be people of joy.

4. HOPE

If hope went away, could you still have a church?

In the search for what matters most, our challenge is to discover how to embody the presence and character of Christ in all we do as individuals and as congregations. Being both divine and human, Jesus wove together the perfectness of God with the struggles of humanity. As a result, his life was a witness of hope. Hope is one of the essentials that matters most if we are to be the church of Jesus Christ in the world today.

It is easy to find hope when we see positive signs around us. The challenge is learning to embrace hope when we cannot see a way through the dilemmas and obstacles we are facing. Many of our churches are declining in the number of active participants and wonder how to turn around that trend. Many are struggling with the changing context of their communities and the world and wonder whether or not they can adapt to their new surroundings. Many are experiencing heightened fears related to the condition of the world and wonder how to remain faithful to a gospel that proclaims hope in the midst of uncertainty. When we contemplate these and other matters, we hope for better days. Yet in the midst of all the tension, it can be challenging to maintain a hopeful spirit.

Life is full of many hopes and expectations. It's natural to hope that a medical diagnosis will turn out a certain way. It's easy to hope that someone will do something we expect without us having to ask for it. It's natural to believe that our way is the right way and to hope that

81

others will believe that way too. We have hopes and expectations of others. They have hopes and expectations of us. These hopes happen in a variety of circumstances and places, including the church. The church has hopes and expectations of us. We have hopes and expectations of the church. Yet when these hopes are not fulfilled, we find ourselves dealing with disappointment, cynicism, and confusion.

"We had hoped that [our Lord Jesus] was the one to redeem Israel" (Luke 24:21). These were the words of two men as they walked and talked with a stranger on the Emmaus Road three days after Jesus had died. They did not realize that the stranger they spoke to was the risen Christ.

These two gentlemen had hoped that Jesus would be their King, their Savior. But their hopes had been dashed when he was crucified on the cross, and they were downtrodden and distressed. Things did not turn out as they had expected, and they were unable to see any other possibility. "We had hoped..."

The amazing part of this story is that these two men were so blinded by their own convictions and perceptions that they did not even recognize Jesus was actually walking beside them! They were so wrapped up in their preoccupations that they could not see him.

This story reminds us that doubts and disappointments are nothing new. Jesus' followers never quite understood who he was and what he could do. They had preconceived notions based on what they hoped for and believed. Though their idea about Jesus being their King and Savior was fundamentally correct, the shallowness of their faith made them spiritually nearsighted. They wanted the kingdom of God to be established right then. They had waited for change and had endured mediocre leadership, and once again they had been disappointed. "We had hoped..."

Our natural response to disappointment is to tell ourselves "we won't get burned again" and to build walls of resistance so that hurt and discouragement cannot invade us once more. The two men on the Emmaus Road did just that. As a result, they could not see truth coming near them, love walking beside them, and hope engaging them in a

82

conversation. The Savior was so close they could touch him, but they were blind and could not see him.

Sometimes in our work to discern what matters most in the church, we allow our circumstances to blind us to possibilities that may be right in front of us. We run the risk of being just like the two men on the Emmaus Road, saying, "We had hoped..."

for a transformed church.
for a certain pastor to be assigned to us.
for a new day of spirit-led leadership.
for the church to turn around its decline.
for people to believe as we believe.
for a change to come by now.
for Jesus to be evident in our midst.

When we gather for worship and Bible study, we hear words such as, "We know that all things work together for good for those who love God, who are called according to his purpose" (Romans 8:28) and "For nothing will be impossible with God" (Luke 1:37). We want to believe, but doubt begins to creep into our minds. Before long that uncertainty dominates our perceptions. Like the two men on the Emmaus Road, our perceptions can blind us when our hope is based solely on our own personal thoughts, feelings, and biases. As a result, we begin to doubt the possibility of transformation and to question the belief that Christ can work in and through all things to transform the world. Before we know it, we begin to think, "Maybe he can. Maybe he can't. Maybe he will. Maybe he won't."

If we are to face the challenges before us, we must sustain our hope. Without hope we grow numb to the voice of God calling us by name, the presence of God working among us, and the power of Jesus being real in our midst. That numbness has a crippling effect on our ability to proclaim and witness to the good news of God's grace, justice, and love. Hope is an essential for effective ministry. Creating hope-filled ministries in response to our beliefs is most definitely one of the things that matters most for the church today.

Something happened to those two men on the Emmaus Road, and they took the bold step of inviting the stranger to join them for the evening. When they exhibited radical hospitality, inviting a stranger in, they recognized Jesus "in the breaking of the bread" (Luke 24:35). At a common, everyday table eating an ordinary meal, they looked into his eyes and watched him break the bread, and they knew it was Jesus. And in their knowing, they once again found hope.

To find hope we often must take a risk. Hope is not found in the absence of conflict. In its best form, hope is found when we open ourselves to see the presence of Jesus in our everyday lives and struggles. The men on the Emmaus Road were amazed to recognize Jesus in an unexpected place. Are you ready to see Jesus in unexpected places?

A few years ago I went through a dark night of the soul, a time when I felt empty and alone and struggled to be hopeful. During that time I had two friends who were on opposite ends of the spectrum in their views. Each could champion causes with conviction and eloquence. Often our interchanges required me to be the referee as I feebly attempted to mediate their two viewpoints. I will never forget the day when both of these friends showed up at my home at the same time with a shared mission project in mind: me. Somehow, without saying a word, they both knew that they needed to reach beyond the issues separating them if they were going to fulfill the mission they held in common that day—encouraging me. They found common ground in the ordinary, and in the next hour I saw the face of Jesus in a way I had never seen it before. In and through them, I found hope.

When our expectations are high and our agendas are focused, we can see in only one direction. If the path we are following is one of gloom, despair, negativism, and fear, then all that we encounter tends to remind us of those feelings. But when we remove our blinders and lower our expectations, we discover that along the path there is a Partner, one who walks with us through our various emotions. And in those moments on the journey when we see Jesus face to face, we discover hope.

A few years ago I received a phone call that I never could have anticipated. A family of four who attended my church had gone on vacation and had been struck head-on by a cement truck that had lost control. All four of them died in the accident. None of my training or experience in pastoral ministry had prepared me for what I was called upon to do. Two funerals were planned, one in our church and the other in the hometown where the couple had grown up. As I prepared for those two services, I prayed for the right words to say and the right Scriptures to quote. I lay awake at night, pouring over how to respond to this tragedy. I was not very hopeful that I had any words that would make a difference.

On the day of the funerals, I greeted family members I had never met. We ushered them to their seats, and the first service began. Songs were sung. Prayers were prayed. Reflections were shared. For me, it all felt so inadequate in comparison to the gravity of the situation. Following the homily, I saw a man in the congregation raise his hand. He was the father of the woman who had died—the grandfather who had lost two lovely grandchildren. As he stood and began to speak, doubts and fears rolled through my mind: *What would he say? How would he get through it? When would I need to intervene?*

Over the next few moments, tears were shed by nearly everyone in the sanctuary. This man who had been confronted with death so unexpectedly and profoundly shared the depth of his faith. He talked eloquently about his belief that this life is not the end of the story. He shared his conviction that God promises to see us through the difficulties of life, never leaving us orphaned and alone. He testified that though he was consumed with grief, his purpose in standing was to profess his faith in a God who loves us especially when we suffer. He told us that although his heart was broken, his faith was not. There were no other words needed. He gave us hope.

On my first trip to Africa, the team I was traveling with made a stop in a rural medical clinic. The open-air hospital was filled with people suffering from leprosy. I witnessed people of all ages and stages struggling with a disease that was decomposing their limbs. It was a gruesome sight. Yet we were greeted with smiles and warmth. A makeshift choir quickly assembled and began to sing for us. The words of the song combined with the expressions on their faces did not seem compatible with the disease they were battling. They sang, "Soon and very soon, we are going to see the King." The words of the song flowed freely from their lips. In the verses that followed they sang about no more crying and no more dying. They ended each verse with "Hallelujah, hallelujah, we are going to see the King."[9] Throughout their singing, it was evident that they believed it.

I was amazed at both what I was hearing and what I was seeing! The smiles on their faces and the joy in their voices overwhelmed me. Later I asked one of the singers how they could sing such a song in the midst of the suffering they were enduring. She simply replied, "If I die tomorrow, I know that I will be in a better place than I am today. I am ready for that because I have hope that our God will take care of us, all of us." Earlier in the day I had complained about the poor seats on the bus and the bumps on the dirt-packed road. Now my complaints were meaningless in comparison to the struggles these patients faced with such hope.

Even today the words of their song and the genuineness of the young woman's testimony bring perspective to my own life and struggles. When life seems to deal an unfortunate blow, I remember that there are those who have faith in the midst of circumstances that are far worse than mine. The words of their song continue to water the seed of my soul: "Soon and very soon, we are going to see the King."[10] And once again I have hope.

God is not through with us yet as a church. While some long for days that have passed, I believe this is our time to make an impact on the world. Will we be known as bearers of hope? Or will we been seen as the generation that witnessed the further decline of the church? We may only dimly see what our role and purpose are, but we are called to have hope that God has been, is, and will be with us through it all.

Jesus brought hope to two men walking on the Emmaus Road. We are called as the body of Christ to combine our gifts and talents in order to reflect the hope of Christ in the world today. As we pray, plan, and prepare to discover what matters most, we surely must fill in the blank with hope. Whether we are ministering to those within the church or courageously taking the message of Christ into the world, others will see Jesus when they witness our hope.

God is not through with us yet as a church. While some long for days that have passed, I believe this is our time to make an impact on the world.

OTHER ESSENTIALS

I had a seminary professor who was fond of saying, "Every moment is a teaching moment." He challenged us never to take anything for granted in our day-to-day work in the church. His conviction was that the church had made assumptions for too long and had forgotten along the way to teach and remind people about the meaning behind some of the simplest concepts. When we assume that we will always know and remember the essentials of the faith, we often fall into behaviors that do not demonstrate what we say we believe.

I am convinced that we are at a critical crossroads in our history as a church. Now is not the time to assume that we know how to cross the street. The traffic is heavy. The vehicles are moving fast. The lanes have been extended. It will not be easy to get to the other side. In order to navigate these uncertain times, it is important for us to draw upon the basic foundations of what we know and be sure that we understand, embrace, and live out these essentials in a way that demonstrates what we profess.

I have suggested four essentials as a beginning point. Rather than assuming our churches will actively live out grace, relationships, joy, and hope, we must be intentional about discovering *how* God is calling us to demonstrate these critical components of our life and witness in today's world. We must ask ourselves questions such as

- Does grace matter in what we do and how we do it?
- Do relationships make a difference in the way that we proclaim God's love?
- Is joy evident in our ongoing work?
- Do we hope for a better day than the one we are currently experiencing?

These four essentials are only the beginning point for discerning what matters most. They point us to the life of God's Son—the one who was both perfectly God and perfectly human; the one who should be the beginning point of any determination of what matters most. As the church, we are to bear witness to God's love and invite others into that love by making and nurturing disciples until Christ comes again. It is our obligation and opportunity to reflect Jesus to the world. To discern what matters most in our public witness, we must examine the one we follow.

As we read the Gospels and study the life and witness of Jesus, let us ask ourselves what additional things could fill in the blank of what matters most—things without which there could be no church. Surely things such as forgiveness, ministry to the poor, befriending the outcast, and welcoming the children will surface. There are others. As you begin the process, be careful to fill in the blank with those things that are driven by the mission and passion of Jesus, not by a personal agenda or passion.

If we are to reclaim our vitality and purpose as representatives of the message Jesus placed into our hands, we must discern and examine the essentials—those principles and passions we are to live out until Jesus returns. In his name, we are called to be the conveyors of things such as grace, relationships, joy, and hope. If we won't, who will?

We are the light of the world
We are a city on a hill
We are called 88 to let our light
came from, going to the light. You are the light shine

5

PADDLING IN THE SAME CANOE

One of the most interesting and beautiful sports to watch is shell boat racing. I regularly find myself in a hotel on the River Ouse in York, England. Early in the morning the rowers make their way along the river. There is no sound of motors and no large wake to grab your attention. Out of the stillness of the morning, a shell boat quietly appears with multiple rowers making their way effortlessly along the glassy water.

What appears to be a simple and easy trip along the river is far more complex and difficult than you might imagine. In his book *The Boys in the Boat*, author Daniel James Brown describes this fine art:

> One of the fundamental challenges in rowing is that when any one member of a crew goes into a slump the entire crew goes

with him.... The demands of rowing are such that every man or woman in a racing shell depends on his or her crewmates to perform almost flawlessly with each and every pull of the oar. The movements of each rower are so intimately intertwined, so precisely synchronized with the movements of all the others, that anyone's rowing mistake or subpar performance can throw off the type of stroke, the balance of the boat, and ultimately the success of the whole crew.[1]

In order for a shell boat to have the appearance of effortlessly gliding on a river, the crew must be intertwined, synchronized, and singularly focused in their rowing. In other words, they have to pitch in and pull together. It reminds me of a favorite saying: "We're all paddling in the same canoe."

Thus far I have attempted to provide a progression of thought and action that will lead to the discernment of what matters most in the ministry of a congregation. The contents of the preceding four chapters are like "oars in the water" that must be intertwined and synchronized in order for you to determine God's call and paddle the canoe with determination and focus.

But what if, as you identify the things that provide the foundation for your church's ministry, the discussion leads to a fork in the road or a difference of opinion around what matters most, or how we are to live out those priorities in our public witness—both as a church and as individuals? This is the overarching question we will explore in this chapter as we remind ourselves how important it is not only to paddle in the same canoe but also to pull together in a synchronized strategy that clearly demonstrates our commitment to what matters most.

THE MORAVIAN MOTTO

There is a phrase often attributed to John Wesley that never originated with him:

"In essentials, unity; in non-essentials, liberty; in all things, love."[2]

This sentence was coined by the Archbishop of Split, Marco Antonio de Dominis, in 1617, but it became popular when the Lutheran theologian Peter Meiderlin used it in 1626 in the midst of the "Thirty Years War." It was during the horrors of this war and the fiercest of dogmatic controversies that Meiderlin's prophetic voice signaled there was a better way—a way of peacemaking that would not stand for violence, discord, or disunity.

Since that time the phrase has been adopted as the motto of the Moravian Church of North America and the Evangelical Presbyterian Church. Though John Wesley never said it, the phrase was chosen as the motto of The United Methodist Church's 1996 General Conference and has been used as a slogan or mission statement on numerous local church websites. This phrase born out of conflict continues to call people of faith to travel a higher road, a road of unity and love.

When disagreements emerge, we can default to negative rhetoric and end up participating in the conflict rather than leading others into peaceful solutions based on civility and grace. When fear and anger drive our emotions, it is easy to lose our perspective and, as a result, our ability to draw upon the essentials of faith that provide peace in the midst of the storm.

There are no simple answers when it comes to dealing with conflict and disagreement, but there are tools that can help us such as this simple phrase. Using this phrase is not glossing over the important discussions needed to discern what matters most. Rather, it is a reminder to reset ourselves with a posture of collaboration, reimagine our role as bearers of peacemaking, reconfigure our minds around issues of unity, and rediscover the depth of an often misused and underutilized word: *love*. Collaboration, peacemaking, unity, and love are necessary if any church or organization is to pull together and paddle in the same canoe.

Paddling in the same canoe requires a singular resolve that drives everyone to use their individual gifts while at the same time honoring the input and giftedness of the others who are paddling toward the same goal. Everyone wins when pulling together around a common goal. Someone may be exceptionally gifted in paddling a canoe or rowing a shell boat, but without the cooperation of the others around him or her, the boat will never reach its intended goal. The crew must pull together in order to reach the finish line!

Every successful organization must find a platform or foundation upon which it can agree. Without a foundation, no building can be constructed. Without a baseline of commonality, an organization will fall into chaos and quickly crumble. The same is true in the church. Our foundation must be made up of the things that matter most—the essentials that give focus and clarity to our mission and ministry. As I've suggested previously, the life and witness of Jesus Christ in the Gospels is the beginning point for determining the platform upon which a church discerns its core values. Things such as grace, hope, relationships, and joy are often assumed postures that can become the foundation for unity, resolve, and intentional action.

But what happens if there is disagreement as we are discerning what matters most? Our society is centered around the concept of a democratic vote using principles such as "Robert's Rules of Order." While this organized process should never be downplayed, a simple vote based on a motion, a second, and a call for the previous question may not be the best way to determine the essentials of ministry.

In recent years a concept called "Holy Conferencing" has been suggested as a model for engaging in civil conversation. This model is based on eight simple yet meaningful foundations upon which to enter into conversation:

1. Every person is a child of God.
2. Listen before speaking.
3. Strive to understand from another's point of view.
4. Strive to reflect accurately the views of others.
5. Disagree without being disagreeable.

6. Speak about issues; do not defame people.
7. Pray, in silence or aloud, before decisions.
8. Let prayer interrupt your busy-ness.[3]

These eight suggestions are an excellent way to frame a conversation around what matters most, especially when there is potential for divergent thought and disagreement. If the opinions of everyone involved truly matter, then the feelings of each person must be carefully considered as well. Jesus mandated that we are to love one another even when we don't necessarily like one another. So determining the foundation upon which a church will build its ministry demands a careful, deliberate, and loving approach.

A loving approach is much more than being cordial or nice to one another. Figuring out what matters most in the midst of many thoughts and opinions is a complex endeavor. As I have emphasized, deep spiritual preparation, reminders of potential obstacles, and intentional reflection on the life of Jesus are critical if we are to set the stage for good discernment. Equally important is establishing and nurturing relationships in order to build trust and care for one another in the midst of important conversations. We must have concern for one another and sincerely attempt to not do harm to others if we are to discern what matters most. Without concern, we become cavalier in voicing our opinions and run the risk of hurting and alienating others who may have a history that informs a different way of thinking—or who simply may not embrace our opinions. As writer Wendy Mass puts it, "Be kind, for everyone you meet is fighting a battle you know nothing about."[4] In other words, there needs to be a certain holiness about us when we enter into deeper conversations.

John Wesley placed a high importance on "class meetings" and "band meetings" for the development of deeper relationships both with God and with one another. It was out of those relationships that friends and colleagues were able to hold one another accountable, encourage one another in love, and nurture a sense of holiness in every conversation.

Speaking of "class meetings," Wesley wrote: "They began to 'bear one another's burdens,' and 'naturally' to 'care for each other.' As they had daily a more intimate acquaintance with, so they had a more endeared affection for each other. And speaking the truth in love, they grew up into him in all things which is the head, even Christ."[5]

Developing relationships is critical if we are to have deep-seated conversations and eventually learn how to paddle in the same canoe even if we don't find mutual agreement on everything. Suggesting that these kinds of conversations can happen when a denominational body gathers only once a year or once every four years seems to be naïve and unrealistic. But suggesting that true discernment of what matters most can happen in relationships that are built within a congregation is much more realistic.

Of course, in the midst of this very deliberate and complex process, inevitably someone will want to paddle in a different direction. This can paralyze any church into a posture of inaction. Over the years I have witnessed churches that will not move into a bold plan of ministry unless everyone agrees. Without fail, these churches never find a way to move off the starting line and paddle the canoe.

When someone will not agree, a clear, courageous decision must be made. Will the group decide to stop, or will they choose to move forward? Will the group resort to a vote, which draws a clear line between the winners and the losers, or will they employ a consensus-making model that increases conversation, tests for agreement, and invites revision?

Inevitably, there comes a point in the discernment process when a congregation must decide to move forward even if everyone does not agree. To reach that point requires some difficult conversations with those who object. Essentially you are asking, "Will you row with us?" Some may decide to do so; others may not. Both of those answers are acceptable if Christian love is the foundation upon which the conversations take place. However, paralyzing the body into inaction is not a faithful response to the call of God to determine what matters most and begin rowing in the same direction.

> Demonstrating how deeply we care for one another
> in spite of our visible differences of opinion is the basis
> upon which a vital congregation emerges. In a world that
> is growing more and more polarized, this may be the
> place where we provide our most effective witness.

Failing to pull together around the essentials dramatically lessens a church's ability to have a credible and consistent public witness. No one wants to end up saying one thing and not doing what we say we believe. Finding the determination to pull together around what matters most and living out that determination with unity of purpose is an exquisite thing when it happens. Our greatest witness as Christians is to demonstrate that we do not have to agree on everything in order to paddle in the same canoe. In fact, exhibiting this deeper sense of unity may be the most enduring legacy any congregation or denomination can provide. I believe that demonstrating how deeply we care for one another in spite of our visible differences of opinion is the basis upon which a vital congregation emerges. In a world that is growing more and more polarized, this may be the place where we provide our most effective witness.

Now, let's take a closer look at this Moravian motto and see if it might help us understand how we can pitch in and pull together to achieve a common goal. In doing so, we will focus on the three action steps suggested in the motto: *unity, liberty,* and *love.* In this chapter we will focus on the first two steps, saving love for our final chapter.

In Essentials, Unity

Unity is defined by Webster's Dictionary as "a condition of harmony; the quality or state of being one."[6] These are the words often associated with what it means to be the body of Christ, the church. We talked in

Chapter 2 about the connectionalism of The United Methodist Church, sometimes referred to as "the blessed connection" that we share. Though that phrase is often used when we talk about apportionment giving or global mission work, it is a powerful part of our corporate witness to say that we are connected together as United Methodists across the world. We share a common heritage, a unified sense of mission, and a core belief that we are to integrate personal and social holiness into our faith. Our understanding of sacrament is that we are, as the Apostle Paul suggested, "baptized into one body—Jews or Greeks, slaves or free— and we were all made to drink of one Spirit" (1 Corinthians 12:13). Taking that a step further, Paul acknowledged that while the body has different parts with different functions, each part belongs to the body so that "if one member suffers, all suffer together with it; if one member is honored, all rejoice together with it" (1 Corinthians 12:26). Addressing a Christian community in Corinth that was fractured and divided, Paul said that there is a more excellent way (1 Corinthians 12:31)—and that is the greater gift of unity.

The world will always show us visions of disunity and a lack of harmony. It doesn't take too many clicks on the television remote to find a station that is reporting the latest example of discord happening somewhere in the world. Those stories provide no inspiration and little hope that unity is possible. If there is any institution in the world that has the core values and belief system to suggest a more excellent way, it is the church. Unity is an absolute necessity for us lest the world deem us heretics and fools.

Jesus spoke to the need for unity in order for the public witness of his followers to be effective. On the night of his betrayal, he prayed these words:

> *"I ask not only on behalf of these, but also on behalf of those who will believe in me through their word, that they may all be one. As you, Father, are in me and I am in you, may they also be in us, so that the world may believe that you have sent*

*me. The glory that you have given me I have given them, so
that they may be one, as we are one, I in them and you in me,
that they may become completely one, so that the world may
know that you have sent me and have loved them even as you
have loved me." (John 17:20-23)*

The undeniable logic of Jesus' thinking in this passage is expressed through the use of two simple words: "so that." Jesus prayed "so that they may be one." He pleaded that his followers abide in him "so that" the world might believe. He acknowledged that he had given them a glimpse of glory "so that" they might come together. And he realized that this unity was critical "so that" the world might know the true love of God.

What this means is that unity is not an option; it is a mandate! Our public witness is greatly diluted every time we display a lack of unity, civility, and grace with one another within the body of Christ. We are called to strive for this more excellent way. It's not that we haven't been instructed in this way. We have. The problem is that often we make every attempt to resort to the easier way by making quick and often hasty decisions as well as declarative statements. Some are fond of using the phrase "it's my way or the highway," which suggests that those deeper conversations that might result in a modified or completely different way are not welcome. Yet to be in community means that it isn't all about me or you; it's about us. To find "our" way is critically important if we are to remain a vital, significant voice for Christ in our communities and world.

Finding this singular purpose and living it out with a common voice is not easy. Speaking of renewal and unity in the church, Dr. William J. Abraham says, "We need all hands on deck for this kind of work. Friends need to take counsel with friends; and enemies need to listen carefully to their enemies within and without their tribal connections within United Methodism."[7] His words ring true. There is no simple way to find and sustain unity. We must draw deep into the well of our souls and find there, at the core, the driving passion for unity that comes from no one other than Jesus himself.

I've suggested that the most essential elements of a church's expression as the body of Christ come from the life of Jesus. Once we have established these core values, everything we do should flow directly from them. These core values are the measuring stick of accountability and the place where we can either confirm we are on track or determine there is more to be done in finding the rhythm of our stroke. Once we have done the hard work of determining what matters most, there should be little to no negotiation around these essentials. The false assumption that arises following discernment is that once the essentials are discovered, the process ends. Actually, fully embracing what matters most requires disciplined rehearsal and consistent practice—not only individually but also corporately as the church.

Have you ever observed professional athletes shortly after they have retired from their sport? For years they bought into the concept of "team" and made endless sacrifices to stay in shape and be mentally prepared. But once those athletes stop their daily discipline and practice, they quickly lose their edge and their ability to perform at a high level.

It takes tremendous discipline and frequent repetitions to stay focused. Step into a batting cage and try to hit a ninety-mile-per-hour fastball. When you strike out, you come to the realization that professional players are good for a reason. They practice their craft. They swing at fastballs every day in practice. Seldom does it come naturally. Frequently it comes under the advice of a good coach. Most often it is a result of disciplined practice—both individually and with their team. And in the end, all of that individual hard work contributes to the desired outcome of being a part of a winning team.

To maintain focus and discipline around what matters most demands a similar discipline. To do the important work of the church and expect it to be easy is to underestimate the depth of the challenge before us. Every time the church gathers, whether it is for worship or a meeting, there should be visual and verbal reminders of who we are, why we exist, and what matters most. Like hitting a fastball, good coaching and focused practice—both individually and as a church—will result in the desired outcome of being a spiritually focused vital congregation.

One of the most anticipated events of my youth was the day I passed my driver's test and went out on my first solo venture behind the wheel. My dad tossed me the keys and I raced out to the car. I put the keys in the ignition and was just about ready to start the car when there was a knock on the driver's side window. It was my grandfather Bickerton, who lived next door to us and had a tremendous influence on my life. I rolled down the window and listened. He looked at me and said four simple words: "Remember, you're a Bickerton." That's all he needed to say. I understood exactly what he meant. He was reminding me that there was a series of expectations in our family—things we were allowed to do and things that were not accepted. There was a standard by which we were raised and lived, and there was a constant rehearsal of these morals, ethics, and understandings. On that day, a sixteen-year-old was putting his family's public witness to the test on his first solo venture behind the wheel. My grandfather's words, "Remember, you're a Bickerton," called me to remember.

Everyone in our church should know exactly what it means to be a Christian and to represent the church's agreed-upon values. The only way to do that is to rehearse, practice, remind, and nudge one another as we embrace who we are, why we exist, and what matters most. It isn't enough to just be a person of strong individual faith. Our ability to transform the world depends on our ability to work in community, with our hearts and minds working in unity around the essentials. If, for example, grace is something that matters most, then there needs to be a sense of unity around the fact that we have determined to be a people of grace. Everything we do should begin to flow from that core value. Why do we embrace grace as a church? Why do we want to be a church of grace? What are the essentials of grace that will give us the best shot of projecting the witness of Christ to the world around us? What are the principles of grace found in the life of Jesus that we should make our own?

As the Moravian Motto says, "In essentials, unity." Any successful venture in ministry requires nothing less.

In Nonessentials, Liberty

Liberty is often equated with the word *freedom* and is defined as "permission especially to go freely within specified limits."[8] Diversity of practice is a norm within the church. To what extent we have freedom has been a topic of active debate and conversation for centuries.

Many point to Acts 15 as a model of what freedom looks like when people of differing opinions discover that the common ground of disciple-making requires diversity of thought and action in order to effectively reach people with the message of God's love. The early church was debating whether or not circumcision was required for salvation. As Paul and Barnabas were evangelizing in the Gentile world and making new believers, they were encountering difficulties when it came to requiring circumcision. When some in the church insisted that the Gentiles must be circumcised, Paul and Barnabas and some other believers went to talk to the apostles and elders in Jerusalem about this issue. After much discussion Peter stood up to make an argument based on an agreed-upon core value and belief—something that mattered most. When this core value was embraced as an agreed-upon premise, it trumped the specific action of circumcision as a requirement. Peter said it simply: "God, who knows the human heart, testified to them by giving them the Holy Spirit, just as he did to us; and in cleansing their hearts by faith he has made no distinction between them and us" (Acts 15:8-9). What was the core value and belief? They believed in the power of the Holy Spirit and God's grace to save and transform anyone's life. As the message of God's love and the active presence of the Holy Spirit spread into unfamiliar regions and began to gain a foothold, the early church discovered that this core belief had multiple expressions and results. Through the work of Paul and Barnabas, they found out that the power of the Holy Spirit and God's grace could transform a Gentile as easily as a Jew.

After much debate, the council in Jerusalem decided that some freedom needed to be granted in how these new believers were incorporated into the church. From that point on, the Gentiles did not need to be circumcised but only to abstain from idol worship, fornication, and those things associated with blood that are offensive to Jesus (see Acts 15:20).

This one event was an amazing breakthrough in the ability of the gospel to be spread to people of different opinions and lifestyles all over the world. If the Jewish leaders of the early church had said, "It's our way or the highway," Paul and Barnabas's mission to the Gentiles probably would not have succeeded. The requirement of complete conformity to cultural lifestyles and regional preferences would have greatly inhibited the opportunity for anyone in the world to accept the message of God's love and the active and transforming presence of the Holy Spirit. Had the Jewish leaders not allowed the adaptation of their firmly held beliefs, it is likely that we might never have had the opportunity to hear the message and believe ourselves. When we study Acts chapter 15 closely, we discover that the religious leaders of the day did not compromise the core values of what matters most. What they did was allow those core values to find multiple expressions in how they were presented and lived out.

Here is the learning for us today. A singular method of presenting the gospel will result in a limited audience who can hear the message. Giving freedom to express our core values in a variety of ways opens up the possibility for God to "accomplish abundantly far more than all we can ask or imagine" (Ephesians 3:20). Our human tendency is to live out of our own scope of understanding and our own vision of what can or cannot happen. This can cause us to put our God in a box of limited possibility. It is safe to suggest that our God has a greater capacity of possibility for how the gospel message is spread than we do. Our job is to open ourselves to fresh expressions of the message and encourage the discovery of new opportunities that are yet to be.

As United Methodists, we are a church of great diversity. Theologically we have conservatives, moderates, and liberals. Geographically we extend from Africa to Europe to the Philippines to Russia to the United States. Autonomously affiliated churches are found in Central and South America. We extend across the spectrum of ages and include people from all political parties. We are a very complex and diverse body of people who make up the body of Christ.

In practice, we embrace multiple forms of baptism, various methods for serving Holy Communion, and untold numbers of ways and times for worship. There is great liberty in the ways we make and nurture disciples. If we were ever to take away these liberties, we would cease to be the powerful spirit-led body of Christ that we have become. This brings us back to a critical question.

How Do We Distinguish Between Essentials and Nonessentials?

Though we've touched on this question previously, the Moravian motto can help us probe it more deeply. Craig D. Atwood, director of the Center for Moravian Studies, says that the Moravian Church has always distinguished between things that are essential and things that, in effect, minister or compliment what is essential.[9] In their work the Moravians attempt to clearly distinguish between essentials and nonessentials. The nonessentials are broken down into two categories— or what they call *incidentals* and *ministerials*.

Incidentals for the Moravian Church are matters of taste, culture, and tradition. They include issues such as whether or not the pastor wears a robe for worship, what type of music is sung during worship, what type of architecture describes the church building, and what local traditions are important.

Many churches get locked into their particular set of incidentals. Pastors who move into new settings and are insensitive to the congregation's set of incidentals can set a poor precedent for their ministry. Without understanding the history of the church and the degree to which that church clings to its incidentals, moving the pulpit to a different place in the chancel area or utilizing a different form of Holy Communion can quickly undermine a new pastor's ministry.

While we should celebrate the ways our congregations do things and the traditions that are important in our life and history, we should not allow the incidentals to be the primary focus for our mission and ministry. Things such as the color of the carpet, whether or not the pews are padded, and the order of the service are matters of preference, which can be changed easily, and not "game-changers" when it comes to the more weighty matters of church doctrine and polity. This doesn't mean that incidentals are unimportant, but it does suggest there are other matters that demand more time, energy, and discernment.

Ministerials, according to Atwood, are sacred tools that help the church by complimenting or pointing people to the essentials of what matters most. They "minister" to the essentials and provide a platform where people can experience and respond to God's grace. The Moravians list things such as confirmation, marriage, rituals, church polity, ordination, clergy, creeds, and the sacraments as ministerials. These things are not incidental, because they lead people to God and provide a vehicle for building people up in faith, hope, and love. According to the Moravians, these gifts are not sacred in and of themselves. In other words, the role of ministerials is to point people to the things that matter most.

When ministerials are being used to cause harm, they can be changed, altered, and improved in their use or application so that they can better communicate the message of what is essential. I am convinced that no well-intentioned Christian would ever want to see a revered church practice used to do harm to any one of God's children. But when certain practices lose their connection to what matters most, those practices run the risk of doing more harm than good. Our goal is to always use everything at our disposal to lead people to faith. For example, as Atwood explains, "Holy Communion and baptism are sacred because they lead us to have faith, love and hope, but they cease to be sacred when we use them to harm or devalue people."[10] So the Moravians believe that a ministerial is judged by how well it leads people to the essentials and can be changed in its use or application when necessary to bring more meaningful, life-giving, and Christlike behaviors to the church.

Essentials for the Moravians represent the "absolute core of faith." If you do not have that which is essential, you no longer have a church. On the other hand, *ministerials* are those things that complement or enhance the essentials. Atwood says, "If the Inquisition imprisoned your bishop, burned your Bibles, closed your church buildings and prevented you from having baptism or Holy Communion, could you still be a Christian?"[11] The obvious answer is yes. Why? Because the essentials of our faith remain even if the things that complement our faith go away.

This is not to deny that we are guided by the efforts of good leaders, inspired by the essential truths found in the Scriptures, and blessed by the reminders of God's love through the sacraments. But the essentials of our faith are the keys upon which we build a vital and enduring ministry.

Using this train of thought, there are things that fundamentally describe the church and give full expression to our understanding of faith—such as salvation by faith in and through Jesus Christ, our belief that God's love is realized in human life through the gift of the Holy Spirit, the essential role of the church to shape us into the likeness of Christ, our belief that God's kingdom is both a present and future reality, and a recognition of the essential role that the Bible plays in matters of faith.[12] Without these beliefs we could not have a church, preach the good news of Christ, or bear faithful witness to the transforming power of God at work in our lives through the Holy Spirit. These are the things that are essential to our faith. But there are a number of things that make up a church that are not essential, such as the style of worship, the organizational structure of committees, the version of the Bible used, the type of music that is played, the type of curriculum used for confirmation, or the particular mission project that is embraced. They complement what matters most in the church, but they do not stand alone as essentials that "make or break" a church's ministry.

It was this very type of thought that influenced John Wesley's theology. Richard Heitzenrater writes,

> Wesley was convinced that believers should be as "fixed as the sun" in their own basic beliefs, but that they should be able to be tolerant of other traditions that vary in secondary matters, such as types of worship and modes of baptism. He would have agreed with the Dissenters of his own day who encapsulated this concept with the motto, "Unity in essentials, tolerance in nonessentials, charity in all things." The central issue for continuing debate between groups, however, is the determination of just where that dividing line between essentials and opinions should fall.[13]

Wesley's words apply not only to our understanding and appreciation of persons of other denominations or faith traditions but also to the various ways we give expression to what matters most within our churches and denomination.

The problem facing The United Methodist Church today is that many voices are arguing that certain incidentals in our ministry deserve a higher place of emphasis and should be labeled as ministerials. Likewise, there is a loud chorus of people arguing that certain ministerials are not nonessentials but are, in effect, essential. Refraining from making nonessentials essential is critical for any church trying to paddle in the same canoe and maintain its focus on "the goal for the prize of the heavenly call of God in Christ Jesus" (Philippians 3:14).

Why do we sometimes struggle to distinguish between what matters most and what compliments what matters most? Often it is because we long for others to be convinced that our way is the only correct way. We want others not only to understand us but also to share our viewpoint. But true success in ministry comes from defining and agreeing on what matters most and then giving freedom or liberty in the manner in which those essentials are expressed: "In essentials, unity; in nonessentials, liberty."

Let's stick our toes in the water and see how this plays out by considering a few important examples.

1. *The Bible and Biblical Interpretation.* United Methodists have long believed that the Bible is essential to our understanding of God's work and continual formation in our lives. The 2012 *United Methodist Book of Discipline* states, "Through Scripture the living Christ meets us in the experience of redeeming grace."[14] If the Bible is essential, then what is nonessential (that which gives expression to the essential) is the translation out of which the Bible is read. Throughout this book I have used the New Revised Standard Version as my translation of choice, but some prefer Eugene Peterson's *The Message* due to its use of modern language and imagery. Others use nothing but the King James Version of the Bible. If we believe there is only one correct or acceptable version of the Holy Scriptures, then we have limited a segment of believers who favor another version. If, however, we believe that the teachings of the Bible can be read in a variety of translations, we begin to pull together in the same canoe.

Let's stick another toe in the water. If we believe there is only one way to read the Scriptures, then we narrow the scope of who will be reached by their message. If, however, we believe and embrace that there are varieties of ways to interpret Scripture, then everyone does not have to conform to our method of interpretation, making room for multiple branches on the same tree. Some ascribe to liberal interpretations of Scripture, seeing the Bible as a story that has life lessons we can embrace. Others take a more conservative approach, seeing and interpreting the Bible more literally. If we can embrace the understanding that both approaches have at their foundation the belief that the Bible is God's word and the source of our inspiration and direction, then paddling in the same canoe becomes more of a possibility.

Conversations around the Bible deteriorate when they center on specifics that we cannot completely discern. But we begin to row together when we discipline ourselves to look for the essentials. For example, rowing together might be determining not to debate over whether or not Jonah was swallowed by a big fish but to affirm and embrace the essential of God's saving grace expressed in the story. Some believe there was an actual fish. Others believe that it is a very important story with deep meaning but doubt that Jonah was literally swallowed by a fish. Putting your opinion aside, can't we all agree that God's grace is illustrated through the account of Jonah? It's possible if we begin to embrace the idea that there are a number of branches that grow from the same tree.

United Methodists believe that the Holy Scriptures are essential to understanding how God has been, is, and will be at work. However, we are a church that is made up of people who interpret the Bible differently. The inevitable questions that arise are, *Where do we draw the line in that interpretation?* and *How can we be unified if we cannot find conformity in our understanding of Scripture?* These are important and emotional questions. Yet in the midst of great diversity, the foundational point upon which we explore and come to a deeper appreciation of one another is found when we are able to embrace a simple concept. People who think differently are not necessarily wrong. They are just different. And they *can* paddle in the same canoe! Without an appreciation of this basic understanding, we will have trouble with the reality of diversity in our midst. With it, we will begin to understand that we can row in the same direction, pursuing the goal of transforming the world with the essential message of God's grace and love.

Let's wade in a little deeper. We know there are conservatives, moderates, and liberals who make up The United Methodist Church, all the while embracing different understandings of Scripture, faith, and practice. Increasing our willingness to do the hard work of understanding one another's biblical interpretations and belief systems can only help our appreciation of one another as well as our public witness as a people of faith. This requires desire, intentionality, and empathy. When we passionately and purposefully work to understand one another, the way history informs belief, how we feel about certain issues, and the lenses through which we see things, a door of wonderful possibilities is suddenly opened. When we enter into conversations with genuine love and empathy for one another, we build morale, motivate excellence, increase our ability to influence others, deepen our ability to wade through conflict, and widen the scope of teamwork. Most of all, we strengthen our ability to bear witness to something that is far deeper than our agreement: our ability to love another in spite of our differences. You and I will not succeed in trying to convert a conservative or liberal to a different viewpoint of Scripture. We can, however, understand one another more deeply and appreciate the diversity that is necessary for the body to be a fuller expression of God.

The struggle in being able to develop an appreciation for the viewpoints of others comes when we are so convinced that our belief is the right way to interpret Scripture. For some it is an unacceptable compromise to accept anything less than "my interpretation." But the real danger in this singular approach is that our minds become filled with our own personal feelings, leaving little or no room for God to occupy that space. To become presumptuous about our ability to interpret Scripture in isolation of communal discernment, dialogue, and discovery is a very perilous path to pursue.

We all should be able to easily embrace the concept that the Bible is the "good news." Holding onto that basic affirmation is essential. But coming to the realization that this "good news" speaks to people in a variety of ways allows God the room to bless others in ways that we cannot imagine. It is challenging and exhausting when we open ourselves to mutual discernment. But when we do the hard work of understanding one another and find empathy for the various positions we hold, an amazing thing begins to unfold: we find ourselves paddling in the same canoe.

2. *Theological Beliefs.* Let's take the discussion a step further with a second example. It is generally accepted that theology—what we think and say about God—is an essential. Scripture informs what we believe about our God. In turn, our specific belief in God informs our approach to living and ministering to others. This link between Scripture and belief makes Christian practice possible. If then our theological beliefs are essential—if they are, in part, what matters most—then the nonessential is the manner in which we express or live out our beliefs.

The Apostle Paul wrote about that in his first letter to the Corinthians. There was great division in the church at Corinth at the time. Divisions were beginning to emerge with debates surfacing over immorality, a reluctance to deal appropriately with one another, unbecoming conduct during the Lord's Supper, misunderstandings about the Resurrection, and favoritism of some above others.

When Paul wrote this letter, he created a baseline for belief. Foundationally, Paul believed that God was their source of strength and had provided for them grace through Jesus Christ that would enable them to be strong to the very end. He wrote, "[God] is the source of your life in Christ Jesus, who became for us wisdom from God, and righteousness and sanctification and redemption, in order that, as it is written, 'Let the one who boasts, boast in the Lord'" (1 Corinthians 1:30-31).

Beyond this foundation, however, there was emerging in Corinth divisions about the way in which those beliefs were expressed. The result was jealousy and quarreling, with sides being taken based on those viewpoints. Paul reminded them that these arguments were not of God but were a result of "human inclinations" (1 Corinthians 3:3). "For when one says, 'I belong to Paul,' and another, 'I belong to Apollos,' are

109

you not merely human? What then is Apollos? What is Paul? Servants through whom you came to believe, as the Lord assigned to each. I planted, Apollos watered, but God gave the growth" (1 Corinthians 3:4-6).

The dispute was over the manner in which the gospel was being expressed. Paul had no use for those human tendencies. He reminded the Christians in Corinth that God provided them with varieties of gifts, services, and activities (1 Corinthians 12:4-6). He helped them to see that the body has many parts and varieties of functions, each necessary for the body to operate properly (1 Corinthians 12:14-26). He affirmed them by recognizing the various gifts God has bestowed on each individual (1 Corinthians 12:27-30). Each of these illustrations affirmed to the Corinthians that these various expressions were of equal value and importance.

What pulled this diversity together, however, was of ultimate importance if the Corinthian church was to preserve its public witness. In each chapter, Paul brought them back to that which unified them in the midst of their diversity:

- "For no one can lay any foundation other than the one that has been laid; that foundation is Jesus Christ." (1 Corinthians 3:11)
- "There are varieties of activities, but it is the same God who activates all of them in everyone." (1 Corinthians 12:6)
- "Now you are the body of Christ and individually members of it." (1 Corinthians 12:27)

Likewise, in today's church there are various ways of expressing our belief in God. We can live with those expressions without expecting everyone to conform to one expression or another if we embrace this baseline theological belief: God's grace has been given to all of us in Christ Jesus and is enriched in him in the ways we faithfully live it out. We make much out of the things that separate us as well as the established categories that define who we are and what we believe. I truly

110

believe that God cares less about our categories and more about disciples making disciples in the variety of ways the Holy Spirit empowers us to do so.

Within United Methodism, there are numerous theologies that drive our understandings of the nature and role of God in our lives. These different theologies or ways of thinking about God have different names—liberation theology, orthodox theology, feminist theology, and systematic theology, to name a few. Is one an absolute? Should our understanding and expression of God be limited to one branch on the tree? Is conformity to one viewpoint essential? For those who believe it is, there is little hope that our church will sustain itself in its current form. But for those who can do the hard work of understanding one another through patience, intentional listening, deep care and genuine love for one another, there will emerge a greater appreciation of differing expressions of belief and a fuller realization that those expressions are necessary for the body to be a more complete reflection of God at work in our midst.

3. *Compassion for others.* I believe that a commitment to caring for the human spirit is essential to being a faithful church. In order to live out our understandings of Scripture and our expressions of theology, we must respond with compassion to humanity's struggle to find the fullness of God. This might involve a different form of outreach for different groups. Conservatives might describe it as proclamation, invitation, and conversion. Liberals might use words such as justice, advocacy, and equality. And moderates might embrace a hybrid of both. Regardless, there are common words and phrases across all theological spectrums that embrace the essential need for us to be committed to one another— words that talk about loving our neighbor, wanting everyone to find his or her way into the heart of God, showing empathy and concern for body and soul, and deeply desiring every human being to experience the essentials of grace, hope, love, and joy. These words cross the boundaries created by our various interpretations of Scripture and expressions of

theology. If caring for all of God's children is essential, then we must build upon that foundation in a spirit of unity by affirming the variety of ways in which God can use us to accomplish that goal.

If compassion is essential, then the nonessential is the manner in which we reach out with the love of God. Whatever the expression might be, at the heart of it is a faithful belief that everyone matters in the eyes of God. If we do the hard work of building trust and relationships, we will not attempt to convert one another to a specific form of ministry but will embrace liberty and mutual respect. Yes, there are various branches on the "care for all of God's children" tree, yet all of those branches belong to the same essential: the belief that all persons are creatures of sacred worth and valued in the eyes of God. Acknowledging this reality allows us to be integrated theologically around the essentials without the various expressions themselves becoming essential. Using the Moravian understanding, those ministries are what give fuller expression to the essentials, but there is "liberty" in how these expressions are carried out.

This ability to explore the various ways God is calling us to give clarity to how we see the essentials is a gift that God has offered to us. There is not one way to offer someone grace. Neither is there a single manner of sharing our faith in God. Grace and faith are essential. In essentials, unity. They are a part of what roots the tree. But on that tree there are many branches, each jutting up to the heavens in a different direction. And on each branch is a flower that turns into a bud, eventually bearing fruit for the kingdom of God. If we depend on all the fruit appearing on one branch, the yield will be far less than if we allow each branch to produce its portion of the harvest. In nonessentials, liberty.

A FINAL WORD ABOUT CONFORMITY

The Moravian motto reminds us of the need for unity in the essentials, liberty in the nonessentials, and love in all things (which we will discuss in the next chapter). This simple phrase can help us pull together and paddle in the same direction. But there's a point I touched on earlier in the chapter that bears repeating, because it is critical to our success in coming together around what matters most. Here it is: *Paddling in the same direction does not require conformity.*

We will not succeed in sustaining the wonderful and blessed connection of The United Methodist Church if we continue to insist on conformity in all things. In settings where complete conformity is attempted, the result is hurt, alienation, and a suppression of heartfelt convictions. As a result, an important segment of the body—one that is needed to express the fullness of God—is left out because of their alternative approach. When we insist on conformity, the consequences are the same as what Paul found in Corinth: a body that cannot find healing, fracturing and fighting that is escalating, a public witness that is severely damaged, and a church that does not reflect the body of Christ as it is intended to be.

In our complex world—where civil government has given permission for things that the church does not embrace; where ministry in other countries is so different and demands a keen awareness of the particular contexts in those settings; where there is such diversity in worship settings, styles, and schedules; where people of all ages, races, genders, and credentials are doing the work of ministry—we can no longer expect conformity in method, expression, or understanding of how we see God at work in our lives. As scary as that may sound, a real beauty emerges from the struggle. It is not a beauty driven out of sameness but a beauty found when we have invested as much time in understanding one another as we have in the preservation of our own viewpoint. It is a beauty found when we discover how to do the things that God blesses, rather than always seeking God's blessing for the various things that we do. It is a beauty found when we embrace the ideas that God isn't through with us yet and there are still plenty of horizons to be explored, even if they are different from the ones we have examined before.

Just as paddling in the same canoe does not require all of the rowers to possess the same gifts, conformity is not an essential for being an effective congregation. With a singular focus and a synchronized or well-thought-out strategy, a church can embrace substantial freedom in the ways that their focus is carried out. We all don't have to like the same things in order to be part of the body of Christ. We *can* disagree and still be friends. In fact, we can disagree and still be a vital body of faith and witness.

In our churches, we have already made up our minds about a lot of things. We have understood and embraced the contexts out of which we do ministry. Collectively we are contemporary *and* traditional, rural *and* urban, liberal *and* conservative, fill in the blank *and* fill in the blank. Using a word from our Moravian friends, these characteristics are the *incidentals.* They are not *essential,* but that does not mean that they are unimportant. Any attempt to move us to a place of conformity in how we live out the gospel would stifle our relevancy, suppress our outreach, and hinder our proclamation of a God who is all about the essentials of grace, hope, relationship, love, and joy.

I remember one member of a former church's administrative council who was highly respected and deeply committed. He also was very quiet. Bill would faithfully sit in the meetings each month, taking in the comments made by the members and listening intently to the various discussions about the ministry that was emerging in the church. As the months unfolded, many new proposals were shared for how we might continue to grow the congregation. Each creative idea was followed by a response from some member of the council. The comments were predictable: "We can't afford to do that." "We don't have the volunteers to make that happen." "We've never done anything like that before." Throughout the debates, which were usually lively and animated, Bill would sit quietly at the table. Near the end of every conversation, he would speak the same words: "The way I look at it, you do what you want to do and you don't do what you don't want to do. If we want to do this, we'll find a way to make it happen. If we don't, we'll find every excuse not to make it happen." After a while, the other members of the council began getting the hint. Bill was simply saying that with the right spirit and attitude, a church can accomplish far more than it ever could otherwise.

Bill's statement was simple but profound. It applies not only to discerning what matters most but also to expressing those essentials—to living out what we say we believe. We do what we want to do. The question is: can we find the courage to do it?

I believe our desire for conformity and for certain nonessentials to become essential is our fear of the unknown. That fear is driven by our neglect in building relationships, our failure to understand one another's stories, and our lack of empathy for one another. How often have you taken the time to truly understand the viewpoint of someone with whom you disagree? How often have you sat at the table with them, inquired about their story, and cared enough to ask about how they came to their understanding? And how often have you done it with such intentionality that afterward your opponent was able to say without hesitation, "You understand me"? The lack of this kind of love for neighbor *within* the church has led to great skepticism beyond the walls of the church about who we are and whether or not we actually mean what we so easily proclaim. What we don't know about one another *will* hurt us—and, in fact, already has. But when we embrace a deep love for one another, we begin to see that the varieties of ways God is using us to build the Kingdom is something we could never conceive of or carry out on our own. We must take great care to ensure that our limited perspective does not limit our awesome God!

The same is true for you and your church. The miracle of God's creation is that no one is created alike. While we can and should embrace a common set of essentials that matter most to us, we should never impede the varieties of ways God might use us and others to fulfill those essentials. It is so easy to point the finger and accuse someone of being wrong simply because he or she is different. It's risky to extend our hands and embrace others. But the truth is that there are good people wherever we go. Good people who are liberal. Good people who are conservative. Good people who are moderate. Good people who read the Bible literally and good people who read it openly. Good people who worship in traditional settings and good people who are reaching people for Christ in abandoned storefronts. Good people who think as we do and good people who think differently.

Can we enter into a relationship with one another? Can we discover a common purpose for the work of making disciples in the name of Jesus Christ, our Lord? Can we find a way to paddle in the same canoe in spite of our differences? In the midst of these questions and many other conversations, there is a quiet voice that may be the wisest of all: "You do what you want to do and don't do what you don't want to do."

Paddling in the same canoe takes a lot of work. But as author Daniel James Brown writes, "Perhaps the seeds of redemption lay not just in perseverance, hard work, and rugged individualism. Perhaps they lay in something more fundamental...the simple notion of everyone pitching in and pulling together."[15] The desire to do it and the results that unfold might just be what you and I are fighting for!

6

Finishing with Love

Having considered the first two parts of the Moravian motto, which focus on the concepts of *unity* and *liberty*, we come now to the final part of the motto: *In all things, love*. Love is the fitting end for our exploration of what matters most, because love is at the heart of all that we believe about the depth of God's mercy, the purpose of Jesus' presence among us, and the power of the Holy Spirit to shape us into people who love God and love neighbor with all our heart, soul, mind, and strength.

Before discussing love as it relates to the ministry of the church, I'd like to set the stage by addressing our basic human need for love. We *all* have the need to be loved and then to share that love with others.

We All Need Love

A few years ago I found myself visiting a newborn baby in a neonatal unit. I went in, put on a gown, scrubbed up, and followed a nurse into the nursery. To my surprise there were babies everywhere! Some were cooing happily. Some were red in the face from screaming. Some looked angelic as they were sleeping. As we passed through the nursery and headed into the neonatal unit, there was a completely different feeling. Here there was a baby who weighed less than two pounds, another who had Down's syndrome, and still another with lung problems. I moved past these newborns and came to the incubator that held the baby I had come to visit.

The little boy was so tiny that I found myself amazed he was alive. There he lay asleep, resting peacefully on his side in the midst of all kinds of medical equipment that was monitoring his vital signs. I couldn't help but stare at him in a silent posture of awe and wonder.

Suddenly the nurse said, "Give me your hands." When I reached out, she handed me a pair of gloves and suggested that I reach into the incubator and touch the little guy. "Oh no," I replied. "I wouldn't want to disturb his sleep or touch him where I shouldn't." The nurse was quick to reply: "Don't worry. We are trying to establish contact with him. You should too! You see, he needs to feel the warmth of your touch."

Before I knew it, she opened the doors of the incubator and encouraged me to put my hands into the tiny, protected crib. As I gently touched this new friend of mine, his little eyes opened suddenly and he looked me straight in the face. It was then that the daddy in me took over and we began our first conversation. I talked. He listened. After a few minutes, I noticed that the nurse had stepped out of the room, trusting in my care as well as my new friend's receptivity to my touch.

When I left the hospital that day, I came to a startling revelation. The nurse was absolutely right. In the midst of the sterile environment and technically advanced equipment, this child needed to experience something far more intimate and personal. He needed to feel the warmth of my touch.

Like that tiny baby, we all need the warmth of a loving touch. First and foremost, we all desperately need the warmth of God's loving touch.

Amazingly, God has always taken the initiative to reach out in love—even despite our unfaithfulness.

One day a long time ago, God reached out in love to establish a covenant with the people who had been created by God's hands. God spoke these enduring words to Abraham: "I will establish my covenant between me and you, and your offspring after you throughout their generations, for an everlasting covenant, to be God to you and to your offspring after you (Genesis 17:7). The biblical record details how God's people failed to live up to their end of the bargain, and the consistency of that story has continued from generation to generation to this very day. God established a covenant. Humanity broke the covenant. Though God has been disappointed repeatedly by that breach, the words from Genesis continue to be the platform of our faith and belief: God promised "an *everlasting* covenant" (emphasis added).

When I think about who we are, I am amazed at the enduring love of our creator God who has had every reason to abandon the covenant and end the relationship. But in spite of our handicaps and flaws, God continues to embrace us with a love that will not let us go. And in those moments when we find ourselves on life support like an infant in an incubator, wondering how we are going to take the next step in the journey, God reaches through the open door and touches us with amazing grace and awesome love. It is in those moments—in the midst of the sterile and technically advanced environment of our world—that we, the children of God, feel the warmth of God's touch.

Centuries after God established the covenant with Abraham, God gave the world another enduring gift to be a pathway into the heart of God: Jesus. He showed mercy to those who were condemned, healed those who were sick, and befriended those who had no one to love them, demonstrating to the world what the warmth of God's touch is all about.

Since the time of Abraham, we have had our own version of what covenant looks like, one that is influenced by our feelings, opinions, experiences, and fears. These factors often create inconsistency between what we profess to believe as representatives of God's word and what we do in response to the hurts inflicted upon us. All too often our lives become modern-day versions of familiar Bible story themes, exposing the inconsistency and misguided nature of God's creation. Our human tendencies of anger, fear, and uncertainty can make us reluctant to extend ourselves into the incubators of others' lives.

Jesus did what we are called to do: place our hands through the opening and gently embrace people in need of grace, hope, joy, and relationship. We are surrounded by examples of the vast difference between God's intention for us and the behaviors we human beings exhibit. Stories of road rage, short-tempered consumers, domestic violence, racism, hate crimes, terrorism, and random shootings make the local and national news every day. In the midst of the tragedy and uncertainty of life, there is the need for someone to reach out a hand of love. In the name of Jesus, we need to offer the world the warmth of our touch.

When I was a young intern in ministry, I had a car that was nearing the end of its earthly existence. Throughout that summer it was in a constant need of repair. Each time the car broke down, a parishioner who owned a nearby gas station repaired it. Whenever I approached him about paying for the repairs, he would say, "The pastor paid the bill." And each time I talked with the pastor about repaying him for his generosity, he would say, "We'll settle up at the end of the summer."

On the last day of my internship, I shared with the pastor my idea of how I would repay all that I owed him over the next several months. He said to me, "I have a better idea. When you graduate from seminary and receive your first appointment, there will come a day when a certain person will walk into your office, look you in the eye, and explain that their car needs repairs and they have no way to pay for it. Fix their car for them, and when you do, we will call it even."

Several years later a woman came into my office and explained that her car had broken down and she had no money to repair it. As she spoke, I'm sure she wondered why tears began to well up in my eyes. In that moment I realized that my turn had arrived. She needed to feel the warmth of someone's touch, and this was my chance to provide it.

We all have a basic human need to be loved and to share that love with others. Love is a critical and undeniable component not only in the process of discerning what matters most but also in the ways we live out those essentials. As the Moravians remind us, we are to love in all things.

IN ALL THINGS, *LOVE*

This final part of the Moravian motto is about inserting love into every situation and context of life following the example of Jesus. When we make love a part of "all things," it is a nonnegotiable aspect of every conversation, debate, and discernment process. When we make love a part of "all things," it is the driver for our devotion and our behavior. Even when we fall short of this mandate due to our human limitations and sinful nature, we make love a part of "all things" by repenting and seeking forgiveness. Love is ultimately what matters most.

Love is at the heart of all that we believe and profess as Christians and as United Methodists. It is the ultimate answer when someone asks what we are fighting for as a body of believers.

One day a Pharisaic lawyer asked Jesus, "Teacher, which commandment in the law is the greatest?" (Matthew 22:36). Jesus replied, "'You shall love the Lord your God with all your heart, and with all your soul, and with all your mind.' This is the greatest and first commandment. And a second is like it: 'You shall love your neighbor as yourself'" (Matthew 22:37-39). Jesus' answer set the standard for every follower since to embrace and follow. He very simply intertwined these two foundational commandments in a way that makes each dependent upon the other. We cannot truly love God without finding a way to love others. Likewise, we cannot genuinely love others without loving God with our whole heart, soul, and mind.

The Apostle Paul understood this to be true. Writing to the church in Philippi, he penned these words:

> *If then there is any encouragement in Christ, any consolation from love, any sharing in the Spirit, any compassion and sympathy, make my joy complete: be of the same mind, having the same love, being in full accord and of one mind. Do nothing from selfish ambition or conceit, but in humility regard others as better than yourselves. Let each of you look not to your own interests, but to the interests of others. Let the same mind be in you that was in Christ Jesus." (Philippians 2:1-5)*

Paul went on to describe his understanding of the way that Jesus lived his life, explaining that Jesus did not exploit the fact that he was God's son but "emptied himself," "took on a human form," "humbled himself," and "became obedient unto death" (Philippians 2:6-8). According to Paul, Jesus entered the human story with a priority and a mandate to love "in all things."

When we have the mind of Christ, his love is the essential core of our being. This was essentially how John Wesley viewed scriptural holiness. Wesley felt that opinions, however right, were only a portion of what a Christian should use as a benchmark for daily living. For Wesley, religion was "nothing short of or different from 'the mind that was in Christ'; the image of God stamped upon the heart; inward righteousness, attended with the peace of God and 'joy in the Holy Ghost.'"[1] This simple reality of the love of Christ within us remains the core belief of the Wesleyan movement and the primary motivator of our mission as a church and as a people.[2]

We express this love that is within us in two directions. The first direction our love takes is vertical, toward God. At the center of our love for God is our belief that God is an active part of our engagement in the world. We demonstrate our love for God most clearly in our devotion to worship, where we lift our praise and adoration to the one who created us, who loves us, and who sustains us by the gift of grace.

The second direction our love takes is horizontal, toward all of God's creation. We demonstrate the depth of our belief in God as creator in the way we care for all that God has created, including our neighbor. The connection between faith and ministries of love is what creates the depth of our spirituality and the breadth of our Christian discipleship.[3] John Wesley insisted that faith must find clear expression in the way we live. His general rules were clear and simple:

> It is therefore expected of all who continue therein that they should continue to evidence their desire of salvation,
> First: By doing no harm, by avoiding evil of every kind...;
> Secondly: By...doing good of every possible sort, and, as far as possible, to all...;
> Thirdly: By attending upon all the ordinances of God.[4]

By ordinances, Wesley meant faithful participation in things such as worship, the sacraments, fasting, and prayer.

In Wesley's rules, we see that love is not simply an emotion. Our feelings of love must be linked to the ways we live out our faith. We are called to intentionally look after one another and seek the good of one another; to guard against the pitfall of not caring for each other, especially when we find ourselves in points of disagreement; to discipline ourselves against apathy and indifference; to battle against any form of hatred; and to earnestly strive to find ways to deepen our love for one another at all times and in all places. This means that we are to combine all our devotion to God with all the gifts we possess so that the depth of our love for God is expressed through the way we love one another. In other words, we are to combine our mind, heart, and soul with our hands and feet in a way that undeniably shows the mind of Christ truly is within us. When we witness this happening in ourselves and in others, what we see is love at work "in all things." In those moments, we suddenly find ourselves sliding our hands into the open doors of others' lives to provide possibilities of hope, healing, and joy in this sterile and technically advanced world. Simply put, the warmth of God's touch drives us to extend the warmth of our touch to others.

When loving another becomes challenging and difficult, it is helpful to remember that we are not so easy to love either. And yet in the midst of our failings and shortcomings, God loved us and loves us still.

Our love must encompass this duality of expression lest it be interpreted as exclusive and meaningless. As we come to a deeper understanding of the love that has been extended to us by the grace of God, we respond by replicating that love for and with others. When loving another becomes challenging and difficult, it is helpful to remember that we are not so easy to love either. And yet in the midst of our failings and shortcomings, God loved us and loves us still. This should cause us to work all the harder to make the love of God come alive in our love for one another. Of course, this is not an easy task, nor is it for the fainthearted. It is challenging, frustrating, and at times exasperating. Yet it is our work—and our calling—to remind the world that in the midst of hatred, persecution, loneliness, uncertainty, and despair, there is a more excellent way. It is called, quite simply, love.

A POTENTIAL CRITICISM

A potential criticism of using the Moravian motto in any discussion of how to determine what matters most in the life and work of our church is that it is too simplistic. We can easily imagine the chorus of naysayers saying, "These are complicated times that deserve more serious and complex attempts to reflect and discern God's will. This is far too simple an exercise to expect any lingering and long-term results."

While it is true that the word *love* is used freely today to describe any number of feelings and reactions, any serious attempt to deepen our love of God and our love for neighbor is anything but a simple and easy exercise. In the midst of serious times and great uncertainty, it is essential that we circle back and reaffirm some basic Christian concepts such as our understanding of how God is at work in the world, our responsibility to devote our lives to loving the God who created us, and our calling to incorporate love into all aspects of our life and witness.

With all of the acts of injustice, hatred, and evil around us, we might be tempted to say, "Why should I care? Given the inevitability that someone, somewhere, at some time will take advantage of my good nature and intentions, why should I attempt to love in all things? What difference will it make?" Similarly, there are those who are hesitant because it seems far too difficult to pull off. After all, it's hard to love some of the time, much less "in all things."

When we find ourselves getting caught up in these questions of hesitancy and doubt, it is important for us to remember how God's grace has been at work in our lives through the witness and care of those who have found a way to make love of God and love of neighbor a reality in the way that they live. It's also helpful to remember how others have hurt us or treated us unfairly, causing us to have doubts and fears about love. Both kinds of memories can drive us into a deeper life of devotion and love. The times when we were blessed can be an incentive to bless others. The times when we have been hurt can help us understand the pain that others experience and be intentional about not replicating that hurt in our interactions with others. In all times, both good and bad, we can remember that we are claimed by a God whose love will not let us go. And with that remembrance, we can go and love likewise.

Years ago I helped create a program to provide renewal for our pastors. The concept was simple: a pastor could request up to two months of "release time" in order to find rest and renewal for ministry. The church would pay for the pastor's salary, benefits, and housing during this time, and the annual conference would pay for the interim pastor's salary and expenses while the pastor was away.

Soon after the program was announced, a pastor requested to participate in the renewal program. I scheduled a meeting with the pastor's oversight committee and made sure to carefully outline all aspects of the program. During the meeting, a man who worked at a nearby plant spoke up: "I'm not in favor of doing this. I wish my employer gave me eight weeks of time away." As he shared, it became clear that he was speaking out of his own hurt caused by the lack of grace extended to him at his workplace. After a few minutes, a gentle soul on the committee looked at the man and said, "Joe, I really don't think you would want us to treat our pastor the way you are treated at work, would you? I think instead that we all would like to treat our pastor like we think we ought to be treated at work." That statement turned the tide of the meeting. The man and his colleagues needed to remember. Some had memories of being treated with grace and respect in the workplace, and this was their opportunity to do the same for their pastor. Others had memories of mistreatment or abuse in the workplace, and this was their opportunity not to replicate that behavior but to treat their pastor the way they would like to be treated.

Embracing love "in all things" means that we take the good and the bad and convert those experiences into a plan of action for living our lives as faithful witnesses of Christ. Though it is challenging to find our way in the midst of great concerns and injustices, it *is* possible. Writing to the church in Rome, the Apostle Paul reminded his readers that the Spirit of God was within them as a source of life to their mortal bodies (Romans 8:11). He also reminded them that the Spirit would help them in their weakness and would intercede on their behalf when they did not know what to do (Romans 8:26-27). Then he shared these wonderful words of faith: "We know that all things work together for good for those who love God, who are called according to his purpose" (Romans 8:28). Both the good and the bad experiences of life can contribute to our strategy for how to make love "in all things" a possibility.

In Hebrews 12 we read, "See to it that no one fails to obtain the grace of God; that no root of bitterness springs up and causes trouble, and through it many become defiled" (v. 15). This verse comes after an acknowledgment of the cloud of witnesses that surrounds us (v. 1)—a powerful source of inspiration and endurance. The writer talks about Jesus as "the pioneer and perfecter of our faith" (v. 2) and encourages us not to reject God's grace as a source of life, power, and encouragement (vv. 14-29). It takes a lot of hard work to resist the root of bitterness that can so easily influence our perceptions of others and our behaviors toward them. As the saying goes, "You can either get bitter or better." The choice is ours.

How we see the world and how we are seen by the world depend entirely on the decisions we make each day. Hear me clearly: it is a *daily decision* to love God and love others. Making that decision requires putting aside some things in order to freely accept and then incorporate the grace and love of God in our daily walk.

On my first day as pastor of a new church assignment, there was a knock on the door of the parsonage. On the other side was a woman who had more wrinkles than I had ever seen on a human being, but they quickly wove together to construct a vibrant and energetic smile. Harriett was a member of my new congregation and, as I later found out, a pillar of the church.

After an initial greeting, Harriett handed me half of an apple pie. "I'll bet you're wondering why I'm giving you only half of an apple pie," she said, giggling. "I baked this pie to welcome you to our community, but on the way here I got to thinking about a family who hasn't been active in our congregation for some time. I just couldn't get them out of my head, so I stopped by and gave them half of your apple pie. I figured that you would be fine with the other half!"

It didn't take me long to figure out that this was the way Harriett lived her life. When I would get a call about someone in the hospital, I would walk into the room and find Harriett sitting there. When I would ask her how she found out about the person's hospitalization, she would say, "I was just driving up the highway and felt led to stop here for some reason." Because of this sense of awareness of the needs of others, Harriett was seen by many as an example of how to personalize God's love by loving others. People would seek her out for prayer and confide in her about their heartaches and struggles. Although the proper definition of a saint includes everyone who calls upon the name of Christ, many people in that community used that word only when they were describing Harriett.

But most people in the community did not know what I knew about Harriett. It was widely known that her oldest son had been killed by a drunk driver years before, but few people knew the enduring struggle Harriett had to forgive that person. She would sit in my office and shed tears over her inability to be all that God had called her to be. Her personal agony was never seen by most, because each day she made the decision to "see to it, . . . that no root of bitterness springs up and causes trouble" (Hebrews 12:15). She made the decision daily to obtain the grace of God and avoid being defiled by the bitterness that so easily tempted her. In the midst of her struggle she found a way to love "in all things."

To love "in all things," we must intentionally choose to make love a part of who we are. What would it look like if we began our day in devotion, asking a basic, fundamental question of ourselves: "How can I love today?" What would it look like if we prayerfully asked God to provide opportunities to demonstrate that love each day?

The most successful worship experiences are those that have a specific, desired outcome. That outcome is the driver for how the service is constructed—what songs are sung, what Scriptures are used, and what invitations are shared. What would it look like if love were the desired outcome not only each time we gather for worship but also for every program, activity, and meeting that takes place in our congregations? That might be the source of transformation and renewal we have been looking for all along—all because of an intentional decision to make love the primary agenda for the life of our church. Just think: a business meeting could be the very place where love finds its greatest expression.

I have been in far too many meetings where there was more concern about the rules of order than the rules of love. Too many church meetings look like a replication of the local Rotary or town council meeting. Business and the proper conducting of a meeting take precedence and become the dominant force in decision making.

What would it be like if our church meetings looked more like church—like worship? That is, after all, who we are. We are not the local civic group. We are the body of Christ. How much time is devoted to prayer in your church's business meetings? How much time is spent searching the Scriptures for links between the work of God and the work of God's church?

What would it be like if all aspects of church looked like heaven? That is, after all, the ultimate desired outcome. If our churches looked like our vision of eternity, we might become more inclusive and less judgmental. If they looked like heaven, they would be places where everyone could expect to find love "in all things."

When we look at the church today, what we often see is a posture of judgment and accusation. In pockets of our life together, we have become very proficient at declaring what is wrong, who is wrong, and why we got into this dilemma. That proficiency has caused us to think at times that we have all the right answers and that the world would be far better off if they just listened to us. As I listen to the eloquence of negative rhetoric that flies so easily across social media, the Internet, and my desk, I wonder how we have gotten to this place in our journey. I also wonder what it will take for us to become more proficient in witnessing to God's love. I have never been overly confident that my proclamations are the will of God, but I am confident that God has claimed, called, and loved me with a love that will never let me go. I am confident that the same claim, call, and love are extended to you as well. And I am confident that, by faith, we can replace our proficiency in negativity with the eloquence of love. Love is the source of our faith and the root from which the branches of our lives grow.

Sometimes we get it right. Sometimes we don't. The biblical record reveals that we are not unlike anyone who has ever lived on planet Earth. We all are just giving it our best shot, trying to live lives that somehow reflect our constant love for God and our deep love for one another. My life is centered on the hope-filled promise that, whether I get it right or get it wrong, God still claims me as one of God's children. This core belief causes Paul's words to the church at Rome to explode with deep meaning and enduring possibility: "For I am convinced that neither death, nor life, nor angels, nor rulers, nor things present, nor things to come, nor powers, nor height, nor depth, nor anything else in all creation, will be able to separate us from the love of God in Christ Jesus our Lord" (Romans 8:38-39).

Finishing with love is coming to the realization that the ending point is also the starting line. Love is the source of our being, the fuel for the journey, and the goal for which we live. God has reached into the incubator of life and touched us with the warmth of love. Will we have the courage to do the same "in all things"?

Perhaps the two connotations of the overarching question of this book—What are we fighting for?—can help to pull everything together while fueling our courage to do the hard but critical work of coming together around what matters most.

What Are We Fighting For?

The first connotation of this question is simply, *Why are we fighting?* There is quite a bit of fighting taking place both in the world and within our denomination these days. Fighting seems to be, for some, the preferred posture. As I have suggested throughout this book, to fight is to choose the easy road of retaliation and rebuttal. To love is to put down our gloves and take the higher road of mutual respect, open inquiry, and constant collaboration. What we often fail to realize is that much is at stake as a result of our fighting, including the negation of much of the good work that the Holy Spirit has accomplished among us. So many historical and present-day stories bear witness to the movement of the Holy Spirit, pulling people and efforts together in a massive witness to what God can accomplish with people like us. The temptation to promote our way as somehow superior to the way of others creates a feeling of dominance that cancels out the good news that there is a way through the weeds of confusion and uncertainty with collaboration and mutual respect. The idea that we might be better off apart than we are together endangers the miraculous mission of the church that is realized when we connect around causes that make an untold difference in the spiritual and physical lives of God's children around the world. The spirit of discord within our denomination and many of our churches projects an ineffective and unhelpful witness to a world that seems to be growing more angry, confused, and cynical each day. The ongoing search of many for the latest example of what someone has said or done wrong overshadows the stories of thousands of lives that are being transformed into something that is right in the eyes of God. As many have said over the years, "An eye for an eye makes everyone blind." But in our eyes, love can conquer all.

The old phrase "when you point the finger at someone else, remember that there are three fingers pointing right back at you" really has some truth to it. Perhaps the lives that most need to be changed by love are not the ones that we are pointing a finger at; perhaps they are the ones that the three fingers are pointing at!

Why are we fighting when we have so much going for us? God has given us the precious gift of the church—and our own branch of it that we call The United Methodist Church. It is our responsibility to take care of it and nurture it. We have been given clear directions and a specific timeline for our work: "Go therefore and make disciples of all nations, baptizing them in the name of the Father and of the Son and of the Holy Spirit, and teaching them to obey everything that I have commanded you. And remember, I am with you always, to the end of the age" (Matthew 28:19-20). Is the latest issue, controversy, or disagreement really where we want to hang our hat and draw our line in the sand? Issues, controversies, and disagreements have and will continue to be with us forever. That is the plight of being human. What we have at our disposal, however, is the possibility of God's dream becoming our own—a dream that the poor might find a roof over their heads and shoes for their feet; a dream that the hungry might be served a sumptuous meal; a dream that the sad might find their burdens lifted; a dream that the loners, losers, and lost ones of the world might find a home in the heart of God.

With all that we have going for us, why in the world are we fighting?

What Are We Fighting *For?*

A second connotation of this question is, *What are we fighting to achieve?* In the emotional climax of the movie *Saving Mr. Banks*, Walt Disney sits across from P. L. Travers over a cup of tea and asks her to give him the rights to her beloved character, Mary Poppins. Mrs. Travers is reluctant because the story is very meaningful to her due to her complicated childhood involving an alcoholic but much beloved father. In this scene, Walt appeals to her with these words: "George Banks, and all he stands for, will be saved. Maybe not in life, but in imagination. Because that's what we storytellers do. We restore order with imagination. We instill hope again and again and again."[5]

These words speak to the art form of storytelling in music, writing, speaking, and acting. If we were to adapt them to our context, they can provide for us a vivid reminder of what we are fighting *for*. We are fighting to preserve the good news of God's love through Jesus Christ. Maybe we don't do that so well all the time, but we do have faith—something that as proclaimers of the gospel we bear witness to in our speaking and our living.

As modern-day disciples of Jesus Christ, we restore order and focus in the church and throughout the world with a faith that many call naïve and out of touch. We believe that there is something more than our experience of life in this world—that there is a more excellent way to live and that God has provided the road map. We believe that we are fighting not only for a preservation of this story but also for a realization of this story in our lives and our churches. We are fighting for unity in the midst of discord. We are fighting for freedom in diversity. We are fighting for love in the midst of it all.

I once had an elderly parishioner who was deeply loved by the young people in the congregation. The children would flock around him each Sunday as he would shower them with love and affection. One day he approached me with the sad news that he had developed cancer and would need to have his voice box removed. What concerned him more than the surgery was the idea that his post-operative raspy, microphone-aided voice would frighten the children. After his surgery, he reluctantly returned to church, deeply afraid of how he might be received. Following worship I noticed that the children had once again gathered around him, but this time he was not speaking with the kids. Instead, he was quietly handing them sticks of chewing gum. The children were thrilled with this new gift, which he gave to them every week thereafter, and they continued to find great support from this important person in their lives.

Several years later when one of those children graduated from high school and went on to college, she quickly discovered all the things she had taken for granted while living at home. She missed her mom's cooking and realized how much work it was to do her own laundry. By fall break she was ready to come home for a visit.

During the morning worship service, I offered the congregation a chance to stand and share their joys and concerns. One by one, people stood and shared a thanksgiving, a blessing they had experienced, or a request for prayer. When I was just about ready to move on to the next part of the service, this young woman stood near the back of the sanctuary and began to describe all the things she now realized she had taken for granted. She wanted us to know that she recognized the influence and impact that so many people had had on her life, and she began sharing about each one. Finally, she looked over at the much beloved elderly gentleman and said these words: "Most of all, I want to say that I owe my salvation to a stick of chewing gum and a man who loved me without ever having to say a word."

You and I live with the hope that God is not through with us yet—neither as individuals nor as a church. We also believe that God can and will continue to use us to "spread scriptural holiness across the land."[6] Through the power of the Holy Spirit—Christ in us—we have the opportunity not only to make a difference in the world but to make the world a different place—sometimes without ever having to say a word.

Ultimately, this *is* what matters most. I have always been accused of being a somewhat naïve optimist. In spite of temptations to think otherwise, I maintain that posture today. I believe that God is not through with The United Methodist Church and its people. I believe that we were created for this time and that we are called to work for the unity of the church, which is the source of our greatest public witness. I believe that in the midst of the fire of struggle, our God will forge a church and a people determined to spread the good news of God's love in amazing and unpredictable ways. While we are, at times, our worst enemy, we serve a God who is our greatest advocate and supporter. There is a way through the morass of our own controversies and struggles. And on the other side of those hardships lies a future filled with goodness and joy.

I believe that is exactly what we are fighting for!

EPILOGUE

Every winter and spring in the annual conference I currently serve, we host several one-day events at our Conference Center for those who are enrolled in church confirmation classes. Our leadership team selects a theme for the annual confirmation events and plans a series of skits, games, and conversations around that theme. During the day I am given approximately thirty minutes to sit on the floor with each confirmation class in a free-for-all session of conversation, including questions and answers. After sharing with the kids about what I do, I offer them the opportunity to ask questions about any subject they would like. Over the years I have fielded questions about topics from world peace to why God would give someone a size 15 foot! It is quite an exhilarating—and exhausting—day!

During one of our confirmation events, I spent time doing my usual presentation. I explained to the students that of all the things I do, sitting on the floor with them is something I cherish most. I told them that confirmation is ultimately a personal decision about to what degree a relationship with God will fit into their lives. I said that of all the decisions they will face in life, deciding what role God will play in their lives will be the most important decision they will ever make. I affirmed how tough it is being a teenager in the twenty-first century with lots of choices coming their way, many forces competing for their energy, and many challenges confronting them such as peer pressure and bullying—both in person and through social media.

Before the students left, I called each of them by name and told them how precious they were to God, to their sponsors, and to me. I reminded them of the claim placed on their lives at their baptism and said that God loved them with a love that would not let them go. I told them that they mattered.

At the end of this exhilarating and exhausting day as I was packing up some things to take home with me, there was a soft knock on my door. Looking up, I saw the head of John, one of the students, peeking around the corner. He said, "Bishop, we are getting ready to leave. I wanted to thank you for spending some time with us. Thanks for the book bag and for the snacks. I really had a great time."

I assured John that I too had had a good time and that I was glad he and his class had come. I told him that he was always welcome and encouraged him to stop by any time he was in the area. He nodded and disappeared.

Before I could gather up my things and head for the exit, there was yet another gentle knock on my door. Once again, John's head peered around the corner. Okay, I thought, I just want to go home. It has been a long and exhausting day.

"Hey, John," I inquired. "What can I do for you?"

"Bishop," he said, "I just wanted you to know—well, I just wanted to tell you before we leave—you matter too."

There was nothing more I needed in that moment. Frankly, there is nothing more I need in the entire journey of life. I had made it a point to tell the kids that they matter, and I was reminded that I matter too.

Growing up, I was always picked last for the baseball team and frequently bullied in school. I was deeply loved at home but struggled to find acceptance out in the world. Though I think I turned out okay, I've always been aware that missing an opportunity to bless someone on their journey can have dire consequences for that individual. On that particular day after the confirmation event, the opportunity to provide a blessing was not missed by a student for his bishop. It was just what I needed to hear.

At times we all wonder what our place is in life. We live in a critical world, where accusations are made and judgments are leveled. There seem to be fingers pointing at us all the time, and it deflates our fragile egos, demeans our sense of self-worth, and leaves us worn out and discouraged. When will it end?

The truth is, it probably never will. That's why deep faith and a strong sense of hope are necessary for the journey. It used to be that people would look at the church and say, "We're counting on you." I'm not so sure they are saying that as loudly or as often as they used to. There is a lot to prove and a great need for us to find a depth of consistency in the way that we love God and love others.

When Jesus stood in front of his disciples before he ascended to heaven, he was looking at a pretty motley crew. They struggled to understand what he was saying. They often resorted to cultural biases and preconceived notions. They were amazed by how he advocated for certain people and were humbled when he put them in their place. They made bold proclamations and seldom were able to back up what they said. Ultimately they betrayed him and watched from a distance as he was crucified. Yet despite it all, he asked them to be his representatives, to build God's church, and to keep the story alive until he comes again in final victory and we feast at his heavenly banquet.

You and I are part of the next generation entrusted with the message of God's grace and love. We are the ones being called upon to determine what matters most so that the next generation can embrace the story and keep the message alive. Like the first disciples, we are a motley crew that can't seem to get it quite right.

I frequently remind myself and others that we are nothing more than a letter within a word within a paragraph within a chapter of a very long book. We are just a very small part of a very large story. But lest we think too little of ourselves, may we never forget that if that letter does not appear in that word, the word does not make any sense. And if that word doesn't make any sense, it can easily disrupt the flow of that paragraph. And if that paragraph doesn't flow properly, the entire chapter can become much more confusing than originally intended. And if that chapter is confusing, it can adversely impact the entire story.

The role that we play at this point in time is a critical part of God's story of love. I know of no person who does not qualify to have the title "child of God." It doesn't matter who you are, what you have done, or what you will do—there is nothing that will ever separate you from the love of God in Christ Jesus our Lord.

Likewise, there is no church too small to be considered inconsequential in the big scheme of kingdom building. I believe that in every state, county, city, town, or village in this world there are disciples to be made. We have talked too much about declining populations and economies and not enough about the fact that the percentage of people who profess no faith is at an all-time high.

All of this is to say that I believe God wants every one of us and each of our churches to play our part in the big story of making and nurturing disciples on the journey. This book has been an attempt to remind us that now is the time to refocus our attention on the things that Jesus told us we should be and do. We will never find complete agreement on any issue, but we can find our focus when we discover God's amazing love for us and the limitless possibilities we have to share that love with others.

NOTES

CHAPTER 1

1. *The Many Adventures of Winnie the Pooh*, "Chapter Five: A Little Black Raincloud," Walt Disney Animated Classics, 1977.
2. T. Jackson and F. Baker, eds., *The Works of John Wesley, Volume 8* (Nashville: Abingdon Press, 1978), 299.
3. Ibid.

CHAPTER 2

1. *Merriam-Webster OnLine*, s.v. "collaborate," accessed June 3, 2015, http://www.merriam-webster.com/dictionary/collaborate.
2. Ibid.
3. Joshua Wolf Shenk, "The Power of Two," *The Atlantic*, July/August 2014, http://www.theatlantic.com/features/archive/2014/06/the-power-of-two/372289/.
4. Ibid., 79.
5. Ibid., 81.
6. This is the current amount raised at the time of this writing; all figures have been determined by the fund-raising unit of The United Methodist Church's "Imagine NO Malaria" campaign, the Reverend Gary Henderson, executive director.
7. Albert C. Outler and Richard P. Heitzenrater, eds., "Catholic Spirit" in *John Wesley's Sermons: An Anthology* (Nashville: Abingdon Press, 1991), 301.
8. Ibid., 305.
9. John Emory, ed., "February 24, 1736," in 1st ed. Vol. 1. of *The Journal of the Reverend John Wesley, A.M.* (New York: T. Mason and G. Lane for the Methodist Episcopal Church; J. Collord, Printer; 1837), 20.
10. Ibid., "January 25, 1736," 17.

CHAPTER 3

1. Gary Mihoces, "The Hardest: Getting Bat to Meet Ball," *USA Today*, March 3, 2003, http://usatoday30.usatoday.com/sports/2003-03-02-ten-hardest-hitting-baseball_x.htm
2. *The Journal of the Reverend John Wesley, A.M*, "March 4, 1738," 62.

CHAPTER 4

1. *Merriam-Webster OnLine*, s.v. "grace," accessed July 9, 2015, http://www.merriam-webster.com/dictionary/grace.

2. Robert Cottrill "Discussing the History and Biblical Themes of Hymns of the Church," "Fill My Cup, Lord," January 3, 2014, http://wordwisehymns.com/2014/01/03/fill-my-cup-lord/.

3. "Fill My Cup, Lord," © 1959 by Richard Blanchard, assigned to Sacred Songs. © 1964 Sacred Songs. *The United Methodist Hymnal* (Nashville: Abingdon Press, 1989), 641.

4. *Merriam-Webster OnLine*, s.v. "Christian," accessed July 9, 2015, http://www.merriam-webster.com/dictionary/christian.

5. G. K. Chesterton, *Orthodoxy* (West Valley City, Utah: Walking Lion Press, 2006), 54.

6. Ibid, 54.

7. Ibid, 158–159.

8. C. S. Lewis, *Letters to Malcolm: Chiefly on Prayer* (San Diego: Harvest Press, 1964), 92–93.

9. Copyright ©1976 Bud John Songs, Inc. Crouch Music/ASCAP (admin. by EMI CMG Publishing). All rights reserved. Used by permission.

10. Ibid.

CHAPTER 5

1. Daniel James Brown, *The Boys in the Boat* (New York: Penquin Books, 2013), 89.

2. "Unity, Liberty and Charity: Building Bridges under Icy Waters," by Donald E. Messer and William J. Abraham, eds., in *The Wesleyan Heritage*, Richard P. Heitzenrater (Nashville: Abingdon Press, 1996), 29.

3. Bishop Sally Dyck, "Eight Principles of Holy Conferencing: A Study Guide for Churches and Groups," https://www.minnesotaumc.org/assets/uploads/documents/Holy_Conferencing_Study_Guide_2012.pdf (Minneapolis: 2012), 3–14.

4. Wendy Mass, *The Candymakers* (New York: Little, Brown and Company, 2010), 76.

5. Rupert E. Davies, editor, *The Works of John Wesley, Volume 9* (Nashville: Abingdon Press, 1989), 262.

6. *Merriam-Webster OnLine*, s.v. "unity," accessed August 4, 2015, http://www.merriam-webster.com/dictionary/unity.

7. Michael G. Cartwright and Andrew D. Kinsey, eds., "Exploring the Past, Renewing the Church: Wesleyan Resources for our Mission Together," William J. Abraham, "Try It, You'll Like It: The Promises and Pitfalls of

Renewal in the Methodist Tradition," page 26, accessed August 5, 2015, http://indianaumc.s3.amazonaws.com /CDCE6B2CD0084065881253EBC082BE87_Exploring_The_Past.pdf, 26.

8. *Merriam-Webster OnLine*, s.v. "liberty," accessed August 5, 2015, http://www.merriam-webster.com/dictionary/liberty.

9. Craig D. Atwood, "In Essentials, Unity: Understanding the Essential Things," Moravian Church in North America, accessed August 5, 2015, http://www.moravian.org/uncatecorized /in-essentials-unity-understanding-the-essential-things/.

10. Ibid., 2.

11. Ibid., 1.

12. *The Book of Discipline of The United Methodist Church 2012* (Nashville, The United Methodist Publishing House, 2012), 47–48.

13. Michael G. Cartwright and Andrew D. Kinsey, eds., "Exploring the Past, Renewing the Church: Wesleyan Resources for our Mission Together," Richard P. Heitzenrater, "Part One: John Wesley and the People Called Methodist in the 21st Century," accessed August 7, 2015, http://indianaumc.s3.amazonaws.com/ CDCE6B2CD0084065881253EBC082BE87_Exploring_The_Past.pdf, 9.

14. *The Book of Discipline of The United Methodist Church 2012*, 81.

15. Daniel James Brown, *The Boys in the Boat*, 123.

CHAPTER 6

1. Rupert E. Davies, ed., *The Works of John Wesley: Volume 9: The Methodist Societies, History, Nature, and Design*, "A Plain Account of The People Called Methodist," (Nashville: Abingdon Press, 1989), 255.

2. See Richard P. Heitzenrater, *Wesley and the People Called Methodists*, (Nashville: Abingdon Press, 1995), 317–322.

3. Authors paraphrase; see *The Book of Discipline of The United Methodist Church 2012*, 52.

4. Ibid., 52.

5. IMDb, quotes, accessed November 5, 2015, http://m.imdb.com/title /tt2140373/quotes?qt=qt2116747.

6. *The Works of John Wesley, Volume 8*, 299.

ACKNOWLEDGMENTS

Early in this book I state that we should collaborate and, when all else fails, collaborate again. Those words most certainly apply to a project like this. I stand in awe of the collaborative efforts of the people who have helped to make this work possible.

I am very grateful to my executive secretary, *Tina Wilson*, for her ability to coordinate my schedule so that I could have the necessary time to do this writing. She is a true partner in ministry, and I am indebted to her for the ways that she makes my professional life more complete and successful.

Much of the research related to the devotional book was the responsibility of my summer intern, *Tori Moody*. I am grateful to her for reading and cataloging countless numbers of my stories that I have compiled over the years. Her enthusiasm kept me focused and hopeful about this work.

This is my first official venture into the world of publishing. This journey into the unknown was filled with curiosity and anxiety. Each one of those uncertainties has been addressed through the timely and insightful responses of my editor, *Sally Sharpe*. Thank you, Sally.

The material in this work has been tested in the appointments that I have been privileged to serve. That is especially true for the time I have spent as the bishop in Western Pennsylvania. The churches, pastors, and people of this annual conference have been so gracious, supportive, and encouraging during my time in this special place. Most especially, I am grateful to the members of my cabinet who have put up with my constant storytelling, especially when they heard the same story on more than one occasion! It is a privilege to work with a team that has at its core a deep desire to discern what matters most to God for our churches.

I am blessed to have someone in my life who is unwavering in her support and encouragement: my wife, *Sally Bickerton*. She is a wonderful partner on this journey of life and ministry. Her love, honesty, and belief in me are the greatest assets I have in ministry. I thank God for the opportunity to benefit from the significant ways she makes me better at what I do. I love you, Sally.

In my heart of hearts I am a storyteller. I remain convinced that the story of God and God's people is the most effective way to draw people into the heart of God. The story of this project would not be adequately told if I were to neglect to acknowledge the blessing I have received from my God each step of the way. My story would never be told if I were not claimed, called, and loved as a child of God.

These are the ones who matter most to me in the story of this project. I am truly grateful for each of them.

The Journey Continues...
Thomas J. Bickerton

What Are We Fighting For?
Coming Together Around
What Matters Most

What Are We Fighting For?
Coming Together Around What Matters Most
978-1-5018-1505-8
978-1-5018-1506-5 eBook

What Are We Fighting For? Leader Guide
978-1-5018-1507-2
978-1-5018-1508-9 eBook

What Are We Fighting For? DVD
9781501815119

Coming Together Around What Matters Most:
A Six-Week Devotional Journey
978-1-5018-1509-6
978-1-5018-1510-2 eBook

What Are We Fighting For? Pastor Resources Download
978-1-5018-1513-3

For more information, visit www.AbingdonPress.com.